THE THOMAS COOK STORY

JOHN PUDNEY

The

THOMAS COOK

Story

London
MICHAEL JOSEPH

First published by
MICHAEL JOSEPH LTD.
26 *Bloomsbury Street*
*London, W.C.*1
1953

*Set and printed in Great Britain by Tonbridge Printers Ltd., Peach Hall
Works, Tonbridge, in Baskerville eleven on twelve point, on paper made
by John Dickinson at Croxley, and bound by James Burn at Esher*

Contents

★

5

6

7

Illustrations
★

8

9

This work
is dedicated
to the abomination
of all that
restricts travel

Preface

SINCE World War II there has been something of a vogue for sponsored histories of Government departments and business firms. This story does not fit that category.

It was a passing reference to Thomas Cook in a book about Palestine, followed by a brief exchange of correspondence in the Press, that first prompted my interest in him. Having an amateur interest in nineteenth-century travel, I looked up references to Thomas Cook, only to find that he had gone unnoticed by biographers. To mark the fiftieth anniversary of the firm, in 1891, W. Fraser Rae had been commissioned to write *The Business of Travel*, an account of the activities of the Cooks and their business up to that date, a volume which was published by the firm itself, but of course was mainly restricted to its history. Excepting occasional articles, a jejune novel and a few paragraphs or a chapter in more general books, there has been nothing else, so, with the encouragement of all concerned, I have endeavoured to fill the gap.

This book was neither commissioned nor subsidised by the famous travel agency that Thomas Cook founded. Any publicity it may afford to the firm, with which I have never had any connection except as an occasional client, is incidental. But I must acknowledge the unconditional access they have given me to their archives and 'museum.' My thanks are due especially to Mr. W. D. C. Cormack, who has been my channel for many facts and recent history, and to Mr. D. Inkpen, formerly the editor of *The Travellers' Gazette*, a Cook publication that followed Thomas Cook's own periodical *The Excursionist*. I am grateful also for the goodwill of the Cook family and for the practical help of Mrs. Frank Cook, Mr. Ernest Cook, and Sir Thomas Cook, Bart.

Above all, I wish to acknowledge my debt to Mr. W. L. Hanchant who has undertaken painstaking and prolonged research, both in such archives of the firm as survived the blitz when, I am told, some three tons of documents were destroyed, and elsewhere among scattered sources.

In addition, I wish to acknowledge my gratitude to the following:

For the loan of books, etc., to Mr. G. K. Wilkie, Chief Librarian, City of Leicester Municipal Libraries; Mrs. Hilda C. Deacon of Smeeton Westerby; Miss Elizabeth F. Deacon of South Kilworth, Rugby; Mr. Charles E. Jarratt of Market Harborough; and Mr. John Walker, assistant editor of *Cook's Staff Magazine*.

To the Rev. Thomas J. Budge, Melbourne Baptist Church, for extracts from the minute books of that church and much other valuable material, and to the Rev. T. J. Hooper, Archdeacon Lane Memorial Baptist Church, Leicester, for extracts from the minute books of that church.

To Mr. F. W. Munson, secretary of the National Temperance League, for access to the League's library, and to Miss Marshall, his assistant, whose help lightened the work of research; to Mr. George T. Bowright, Chairman of the Merseyside Band of Hope Union, and Mr. Michael Keeley, general secretary of the Leicester Temperance Society, for much helpful information.

To those who kindly replied to requests for information made in the correspondence columns of the Press, and to others including the Rev. Ernest A. Payne, M.A., D.D., general secretary of the Baptist Union of Great Britain; the Rev. E. J. Tongue, B.A., D.D., secretary of the Bristol Baptist College; Mr. H. L. Hemmens, editor of the Baptist Missionary Press; and Mrs. Audrey M. Woodcock, Leicester City Archivist.

CHAPTER ONE

The Household Word

IT was a July day which seemed to belong to the English Midlands. Hot but not sunny. Wind fretted beneath a leaden sky: the summer afternoon was landlocked, sultry, there at England's centre, where press photographers trampled a small, thirsty garden enclosed by thick hedges. The photographers stood upon kitchen chairs anxiously endeavouring to get a slant, within the confined space, upon the uncompromisingly plain brick front of a semi-detached cottage. There was room only in the garden —and in the picture—for the Chairman of the Parish Council, the Baptist Minister and the Man-from-London. People from the Midlands closed in round the necessarily cramped, dignified but obscure ceremony; so far from the sea, from capital cities, from the international highways of the world. Prayers were offered. The sun gleamed briefly. A drape fell away, obediently, languidly, to reveal a plain bronze tablet put on the birthplace of Thomas Cook in Melbourne, Derbyshire. In accord with the unostentatious surroundings they had inscribed the simple words *He made world travel easier* upon the plaque commemorative of the Melbourne lad whose name became a household word throughout the world.

Afterwards, in that crowd of stolid, undemonstrative Midland folk, many of whom had never set foot outside their own country—and some indeed never outside their native place—I met several who recollected Thomas Cook himself, old, silk-hatted, blind and ailing, driving in a carriage and pair out of the great sophisticated world of international travel to revisit with characteristic nineteenth-century attitude the place of his birth. He was carried, they told me, into one of the fourteen almshouses that he had caused to be erected, adjoining the Memorial Hall where we took a meat and strawberry tea after the unveiling. He had shed tears when he realized how many steps and stairs his architect had built for those 'poor and deserving persons belonging to the General Baptist Denomination' who still pay one penny a week for their accommodation. The steps and stairs remain, and personal memories linger yet of this phenomenal son of the Midlands who was born up the road in 1808 and who died a few miles away in Leicester in 1892, having carried his name to the ends of the earth and organized even the travels of his sovereign, Queen Victoria.

He left behind him a name which has passed into every language and a unique business which still serves millions of passengers. His modest estate was sworn at £2,497 1s. 6d. His son, when he died seven years later, left an estate valued at £663,534.

The business, which makes travel arrangements for some ten million people a year, continued to be owned by the Cook family until the late nineteen-twenties, when it became associated with the Continental enterprise known to most English-speaking people as the International Sleeping Car Company and to the Continent as Wagons-Lits. In World War II the interests of this Company, which was registered in Belgium, passed into the control of the British Custodian of Enemy Property, from whom it was acquired by the four main-line British Railways, subject to certain reservations concerning the interests of the Wagon-Lits which were to be handed over to that Company on the termination of hostilities.

Subsequently, when British Railways were nationalized, the British portion of Cooks' interests owned by the Railways was taken over by the British Transport Commission. In their report dated 1948, the Commission stated that 'the specialized activities of this Company, which naturally link closely with the transport facilities of the Commission, have continued to be carried on successfully and efficiently under this decentralized direction.'

Bewildered as well he may have been by the jargon of this century, the ghost of old Thomas Cook may well have got some satisfaction from the report. The profit of the undertaking as a whole owned by the Commission and the International Sleeping Car Company, was stated to be approximately £600,000 in a single year.

Ten thousand employees of various nationalities throughout the world still serve that plain and cherished name—a family name no matter what jargon obscures its real nature. Three hundred and fifty branches in sixty countries, including those of associated and subsidiary companies, I am told, is the present score. That exemplary local-boy-made-good, that strict moralist, that God-fearing epitome of Victorian enterprise, that worthy, almost great, opportunist, so much a product of his times yet withal so great an influence upon them, would have revelled in such figures. Thomas Cook was never inarticulate or unforthcoming with statistics. Indeed, for one who spoke no language but his own—and used, as my Melbourne witnesses tell me, not the smooth speech of the ruling classes of his time but the unadorned accent of Leicester— he was prodigiously eloquent. His tenacity of the principles and the practice of Good Work and Good Business was tireless, and he was ever ready to take the opportunities which the nineteenth century so abundantly offered. Thomas Cook was a stern apostle of righteousness, but he was no stick-in-the-mud. His Memorial Cottages and the plaque at Melbourne cradled in the thriving, unpretentious, landlocked Midland landscape serve as reminders of the man of principle. The organization which bears his name and deals with logistics unimagined in his spacious, steam-powered world is an ever-active memorial to his enterprise. In the Berkeley Street headquarters in London, where, no doubt, his statistical ghost takes pride in the five thousand telephone calls a day and the forty tons of mail a year, the very floor directory is a tribute to the man. There is the *Eastern Princes Dept.* still handling Highnesses amid the democratic turmoil of mass travel— for did not Cook first organize their forbears when they first made their elaborate journeys to Britain to pay tribute to the Queen Empress? There is the *Pilgrimages Dept.*—for did not Cook make one of his famous 'arrangements' for pilgrims to travel to Mecca as far back as the eighteen-eighties. No doubt the *Film Location Dept.* would puzzle him at first: and I wonder if he would have approved the change of title which turned the *Aerial Dept.*—so suggestive of Montpelier—into the *Air Travel Dept.* where the customer can now choose between hover-plane and jet.

Thomas Cook himself, no mean hand at a cliché, has, of course, been described not only as The Peerless Excursionist, but also as The Patron Saint of Travel. Judging by some of the correspondence files which I have explored, he and his successors have been regarded as an earthly embodiment of omniscience and omnipotence. This from Bournemouth, for instance: *Can you tell me where a British subject can find peace from a fiend of a wife who has ample means of her own? Should like a mild climate, moderate cost of living and plenty of fruit.* A faded copy of the reply tells me that the sufferer was invited to call at the office which 'will be very pleased to give you advice on the points raised by you'—but there, alas, the file tantalizingly closes.

A Californian orange-grower wrote: *I have been instructed by my daughter to address letters to her, care of you or your son. I presume either one will do as it is the same address. I wish you would take this matter up with her when she calls for her mail and get this matter spread around . . . and if you ever come to California,*

U.S.A., I'll get you the key of the State Treasury, and show you around . . .

To the old headquarters at Ludgate Circus came this note from one Acha Baba of Calcutta about a son: *Sir,— I crave of you but a few moments: My son Ali has just failed to pass his Matric., but he is at running excellent, at gymnastics very wonderful, and at weight-lifting a Goliath. Would you please to consider him as a candidate for your Ludgate Circus? For which act of kindness I shall ever pray for your long life and prosperity.* From the city of Norwich a request, well calculated to tax the omniscience of a Pillar of Temperance: *I am trying to ascertain where a particular brand of whisky may be procured which is sold abroad—a sketch of the bottle seal is on the opposite page.*

More than fifty years after his death the demands of the eccentric are still usually addressed to Thomas Cook in person. Simple requests for matchbook covers, for *the exact populations of London and New York,* for whist-drive score cards (in aid of an East Coast church restoration fund), even for the address of someone in Thibet *to whom I might write for information concerning the present situation,* are easy enough to deal with. More ingenuity is required to trace temporarily lost or long-missing persons. Yet the firm has done this. One lady, in 1939, wrote: *Our daughter . . . is on Tour 15 somewhere in Russia. It is her birthday to-morrow, the 15th, and I want to get a telegram through to reach her . . .* The daughter was certainly not on a Cook's Tour, but the firm traced her as one of a party organized by Intourist, the Russian official travel agency, and the birthday message was promptly cabled.

An elderly egoist, in the middle of World War II, waged a long correspondence in an effort to secure a Continental holiday as she had been having trouble with her grand-daughter and wanted to get as far away as possible from that young woman. A pencilled letter from a Durham Lad, 1941, reads: *My ambition is to be a film star . . . My parents wanted me to go down the pits . . . so I ran away . . .*

would you help me to get across to Canada or America . . . If I do not get across I shall go mad . . . Others have different ambitions. A Dutchman, in 1938, wrote declaring himself *an admirer of English culture and English women. With a view on . . . possible marriage I would like to reside for a fortnight or three weeks in a boarding-house (middle to good-class) in a popular holiday resort in England, by joining which, I have the largest possible occasions to meet young English ladies of well-to-do, and esteemed, families, till 25 or 28 years of age . . .* I consider the firm's reply a model of helpful discretion.

The West Coast of Africa is an unfailing source of entertaining correspondence. In 1938, a self-described 'Merchant Prince' of the Gold Coast sought to do business with the 'Jerusalem branch' in a Masefieldian cargo of *Ivory, Prodice, Mahogany and Fancy Goods.* About the same time, a native choirmaster asked for a *catalogue of Surplices, Cassocks, Organists Surplices and gowns outfits for lady Chorister, etc.* But the most endearing and characteristic of the letters from these parts is the following:

I want to tell you that I want to make friend with you Please sent me fountain pen and some books which will read. I hope that you will do so. God bless you and your wife . . .

I offer such examples not even as a frivolous testimonial to the man and his business, but rather as an indication of the ubiquity of an almost legendary reputation which so surprisingly accrued to the firm founded on ideals nurtured in the semi-detached cottage in Quick Close. It is a reputation very characteristic of its age: and its dimension is that of worthiness rather than greatness. Cook's death in the 'nineties, immediately followed the celebration of his Jubilee in Good Business, rated a leader in *The Times.* His obituaries, like his own writings, were eloquent to the point of verbosity. *The Times,* it seems to me, even at that distance, brought at least the commercial aspect of the Cook reputation into reasonable focus. Let me be for-

given, therefore, if I seem to put the cart before the horse
in quoting at the beginning of my study of the man, his
son and their work, this brief assessment of him at the
time of his death.

'The late Mr. Thomas Cook . . . was a typical middle-
class nineteenth-century Englishman. Starting from very
small beginnings, he had the good luck and the insight to
discover a new want, and to provide for it. He saw that
the great new invention of the railway might be made, by
the help of a new organization, to provide large numbers
of people with pleasanter, cheaper, and more varied
holidays than they had ever been able to enjoy before.'

Referring, later, to father and son, the leader-writer
continued: '. . . They have organized travel as it was never
organized before, and they have their reward in the
enormous increase in the number of travellers, of whom so
many come to them for help. Much credit is due to the
late Mr. Thomas Cook, the founder, and to his son, the
consolidator of the business—the Julius and the Augustus
Cæsar of modern travel. They have applied the resources
of civilization to a very general modern need, and for this
they deserve and obtain full recognition. If on occasions
like the jubilee last year, their friends are a little inclined
to take a too lofty view of this service to humanity, such a
natural exaggeration is easily pardoned.'

CHAPTER TWO

From Sixpence
to Ten Shillings a Week

IN quest of Thomas Cook, it seems only proper that we should arrive by rail; but, alas, the line from Derby to Melbourne, opened in the eighteen-sixties when the Peerless Excursionist was already a name to conjure with, has carried no passenger traffic for a quarter of a century. The old railwaymen to whom Cook's stately arrivals in his later years are a cherished memory, have long since retired. One who spoke to me with such loving nostalgia of the great steam days of Cook had himself travelled into Melbourne by one of the many bus services which crowd the roads in those parts where steam is already redundant for shorter journeys.

However we cover the ground, historic associations assert themselves as we journey from Derby to Melbourne, enjoying a landscape little changed since Thomas Cook made his earliest journeys over that road by the means to which he liked to refer as 'Shank's naggie.' We cross, as he did, the long Swarkstone bridge, spanning the Trent, which was the most southerly point reached by the vanguard of the Young Pretender's army in 1745. The bridge was already five hundred years old then. Some of the thirteenth-century stones which carry this century's main road may have been familiar to Robin Hood who, if he lived at all, may well have been born, as legend says, at nearby Chellaston.

Thomas Cook never lost his love for this native country-side of his, and no doubt it influenced his expressed ideals when, later in life, he set up in business as a travel agent. He wanted others to share his enjoyment of natural beauty and historic places. He regarded it as his mission to make this enjoyment available to all at a cost the humblest might afford.

Already on the outskirts of Melbourne we are amidst the market-gardens, watered by streams meandering towards the Trent, which for long have provided a livelihood for many of the people of the place and enjoy such repute that 'Melbourne grown' is a recommendation for produce throughout the Midlands, and indeed in London's Covent Garden itself. We enter the plain little town of growers and manufacturers whose population remains steady at about four thousand and sense something of the history of almost a thousand years. A contrast to its Australian sister, with little more than a century's history, yet already with a population expanding towards a million and a half. How incredulous would have been the youthful Thomas Cook had he been told that, in a then undreamed-of antipodean city bearing the name of his own birthplace, there would be opened, before his death, one of a chain of offices conducting the business of a great world-encircling enterprise bearing his name, that, moreover, when a commemorative tablet was unveiled on his birthplace, the Australian Lord Mayor would cable the Chairman of the Parish Council making that 'the opportunity to extend to you cordial and warm greetings from your namesake here in Australia.' The capital of Victoria was not, of course, directly named after the Derbyshire town, but in compliment to Lord Melbourne, whose title derived from the great house of the place, Melbourne Hall. When the Australian city celebrated its centenary, a message was sent from Melbourne, Derbyshire, which proudly reminded the greater place: 'Our little town . . . was mentioned in Domesday Book, in which it is stated there was a priest and a church and a mill of three shillings and twenty-four acres of meadowland. The church stands to-day as one of the finest Norman churches in England, and there is a water-mill still occupying the site of the old one . . .'

The valley town, set amidst gentle hills crowned with limes and elms and sycamores, has other memorials of the past, though only a fragment or so remains of Melbourne Castle, to which the Duke of Bourbon was brought, to endure his nineteen-years' captivity after Agincourt. It is said that the stone from which the Castle was built came from a quarry now filled by Melbourne Pool. Facing that water, which provides a noble rink in winter, stands Melbourne Hall, its modest grandeur supported by fifteen acres of formal gardens. These are famous for their terraces and lawns, for their cedars, limes and pines, for their fountains and lead statues, for the summer-house in wrought-iron filigree, for stately yew hedges and, most of all, for that local wonder of the world a yew tunnel a hundred yards long. All this is eloquent of an aristocratic way of life, of the pleasures of privilege enjoyed by such as the families of Coke and Lamb and Kerr to which in succession it has belonged. Perhaps their most notable owner was William Lamb, that second Viscount Melbourne, who found it 'a damned bore' to be Prime Minister of England.

By way of contrast, let us turn toward No. 9 Quick Close, at the working end of this town of contrasts, to the square, unmellowed cottage that suggests generations of humble lives spent in struggle against privation, if not against downright poverty. Millions who remember little of the noble lord of the Hall, except his scarce-distinguished place in the role of those who have held the same high office, yet recognize the name of Thomas Cook who was born in this humble place on November 22nd, 1808.

His parents, John Cook and Elizabeth Perkins, had been married in the previous February, at Melbourne parish church. It is obvious that both were in humble circumstances. John Cook's occupation is unknown. Elizabeth, his wife, although she could not write and had to sign the marriage register with her mark, was the eldest of the three daughters of Thomas Perkins who, for thirty years, from 1760 to 1790, was co-pastor with Francis Smith, of the Melbourne General Baptist Church.

It is probable that young Thomas inherited something of the character as well as the Christian name of grandfather Thomas Perkins. This local worthy lived at Hinckley as a young man, and there attended the Baptist services begun by William Ault in 1748, being one of the earliest of the Hinckley converts. Himself imbued with proselytizing zeal, and being possessed of 'fair mental ability, good health, somewhat of boldness, a good voice and fluency of speech,' he soon was recognized as a preacher of the 'hell-fire' school. The Rev. Thomas J. Budge, the present Baptist Minister at Melbourne, quotes a description of him in debate: 'Thomas Perkins . . . had come with boiling enthusiasm, and in tones of thunder, to hurl verses and paragraphs of the sacred writings like huge boulders to crush down all opponents.' In 1760, Perkins was ordained joint minister with Francis Smith at Melbourne, removing thence from Hinckley. For a long while his ministry was highly successful. 'But about the year 1785, and when somewhat advanced in life, he contracted a marriage which was thought by many of the friends to be an imprudent one, and which led to his retirement from the ministry.' His death took place in January, 1792, as the result of falling downstairs.

Such was Thomas Cook's maternal grandfather. His daughter, Elizabeth, could not have been more than five or six years old at the time of his death, but, despite the imprudency of her father's marriage, she would seem to have been brought up with a degree of strictness, if we may judge from her own concern for her soon fatherless son. For John Cook died in 1812, and was buried in the neat Baptist graveyard in the middle of Melbourne town. There was no money to spare for a stone in a family whose pence were needed for bread. The hardships of her widow's life may have influenced Elizabeth Cook's decision to make a second marriage. On September 14th, 1812, she again made her mark in the marriage register at Melbourne and became the wife of James Smithard.*

His stepfather seems to have encouraged Elizabeth in her care for young Thomas. The couple gave the boy such schooling as they could afford. It is possible that his mother would have had him be a Baptist minister as her father was. At all events, he was grounded in the elements of an ordinary education by three men of 'stern integrity and religious character—T. Pickering, John Smith and Joseph Tagg.'

Elizabeth bore two sons to Smithard, Simeon and James; and it was with the advent of Simeon, in 1818, that the problem of an extra mouth had to be solved by taking Thomas from school. Even the scanty earnings of the ten-year-old boy were needed to help the family resources. How slender those resources were is suggested by his earnings of sixpence a week from one of the local market gardeners, John Roby.

It is said that the slim-built, active little boy won the esteem of his master, with whom he worked for about four years. This esteem was not altogether reciprocated. For Roby, though a member of a religious body, sometimes returned the worse for drink from the marketing of his produce. His sons followed their father's example. Hence, willy-nilly, the young Thomas Cook, when not more than twelve years old, had to go the rounds of the neighbouring villages crying 'Peas! Beans! Seeds! Plants for sale!' or

* There is a previous entry in the register of James Smithard having married Ann Hollingsworth, March 28th, 1802. It would therefore appear that Smithard was both a widower and older than his second wife.

was sent to stand in the market-place at Derby hawking
fruit and vegetables—he who was to girdle the world with
his business.

When Thomas was about fourteen years old, in 1822,
it was decided that he should be indentured to his uncle,
John Pegg, a wood-turner and cabinet-maker who had
married his mother's sister Ann. As a reward for steady
application, he gradually acquired a skill, not only with
the lathe but in other aspects of the turner's and cabinet-
maker's craft. Yet his new work was often as tedious as his
job with the gardener had been. He learnt the drudgery
of ripping ashplanks with a handsaw into the pieces from
which farm-tool shafts were turned. To get through his
stint and later have some time for fishing in the Trent, his
favourite pleasure, he would often begin work at two or
three in the morning, keeping himself going on a little
milk saved from overnight. These industrious habits must
have been native; they seem to have owed little to the
example of his master. 'The turner sought his relaxation
and enjoyment night after night,' to quote a possibly
biased account from *The Temperance Mirror*, of 1889, 'in a
snug corner in the village public-house, where much of his
time was wasted and his means so dissipated that, not-
withstanding a good business, he lived and died a poor
man.'

The thoughts of Thomas Cook were beginning to turn
towards the evil of strong drink. They were never to be
deflected. His apprenticeship to Pegg lasted for a term of
five years, during which his mother's means had again
become straitened. I am inclined to think that his
stepfather had died just before the beginning of his articles,
and that his apprenticeship, which of course implied
'living-in,' was a practical family attempt to ease his
mother's difficulties. She herself, with Thomas's two young
step-brothers to provide for, now decided to open a
small shop where, with some help from Thomas, she might
sell earthenware and books—an unusual combination

explicable, to some extent, by an influence which helped to bring about a more significant event.

On December 18th, 1825, so the minute-books of the Melbourne Baptist Church record, Thomas Cook and three others 'were proposed for baptism and fellowship.' In the following February, three months after his seventeenth birthday, Thomas was 'duly' baptised and welcomed into the fellowship of the church. He had made his decision, of course, in the deep sincerity of his personal convictions. But he had been helped to that decision by at least two other people. He had been brought up with the example of his mother's devotion to her Church constantly before him. In his impressionable years he had also come under the evangelical sway of the remarkable J. F. Winks,* who was minister at Melbourne for two years.

Winks influenced the young Thomas Cook in more than the matter of his baptism. It had been revealed to the minister himself during his short term at Melbourne, that his lifework was to be 'the supplying of Baptist Sunday schools and churches with cheap and appropriate periodical literature.' He had indeed already set up a printing press at Loughborough, whence he finally removed from Melbourne in 1826 to become a publisher to the General Baptist Association. After a subsequent removal to Leicester, Winks continued for nearly forty years to edit and publish magazines 'for the young and poor.'

Here then is a clue to the presence of books in the illiterate Mrs. Smithard's earthenware shop. Probably the venture was also made to serve as a 'repository' for Baptist publications, periodicals, tracts and pamphlets,

---

* Born at Gainsborough in 1792, Winks had been converted when a draper's apprentice at Retford and had begun to teach and preach after his return to his native town as a draper's assistant. He became pastor of the small church of Killingholme but accepted a call to Melbourne in 1824. Later, although managing his large business as a printer and publisher and heavily engaged in editorial work, he also served as unpaid minister of the Carley Street Church at Leicester from 1839 to 1860, and for two years subsequently of the Church at Market Harborough.

the presence of which suggests not only the influence of
Winks, but a new and increasingly urgent interest on the
part of Thomas Cook.

Accounts of this period of his life are meagre and do not
altogether tally. At least one suggestion is that his apprenticeship was never completed owing to the unsatisfactory
conduct of Pegg. Possibly he found employment for a
while as assistant to Winks at Loughborough, though
their business association may have been limited to the
supplying of stock by Winks to be sold on commission in
the little Melbourne shop or for Cook to distribute on his
journeys as a village evangelist. Heredity will out. Thomas
Cook had become moved with a missionary fervour, much
as his grandfather, Thomas Perkins, had been, and thus
was far from wholly satisfied by work in the Melbourne
Sunday school.

There was his friend John Earp—a surname still wide-
spread and prolific in these parts. John Earp, born at
Melbourne in 1804, was later compelled by circumstances
to give up his training as a surgeon and became a wool-
buyer and maltster. He was a lifelong zealous worker in
Baptist causes, and one of a deputation to the King of
Denmark, in 1857, to plead on behalf of the persecuted
Baptists in that country.

Earp was not baptised and received into the church
until a year later than Thomas Cook, but together they
began to tramp the countryside as village evangelists. It
was essential to the success of this work that they should
become fluent and practised speakers. The pair of them
therefore used to climb through the windows of the
Melbourne chapel in the early hours of the morning, each
in turn playing preacher and congregation. During World
War II those windows were demolished, so that such a
zealous feat may seem a little far-fetched to succeeding
generations who see only the replacements. Their acro-
batics, however, seem to have been successful, and their
work prospered. In 1828, the Midland General Baptist

Churches decided to renew their home mission endeavours. The minute book of the Melbourne Baptist Church contains an entry, October 20th, 1828: 'It was agreed that Brother Nailor* should send a letter to the committee of the Home Mission, in behalf of Brother Cook, as a recommendation, so far as regards his piety—and as a suitable person for the important work of an Evangelist, so far as we judge him fit, what other qualifications are requisite we as a Church not knowing the extent of the work devolving on a person in that station, we leave the case to the discretion and judgment of the committee.'

The committee approved of Cook and he was appointed evangelist. A solemn service of dedication was held at Melbourne and the young evangelist took up his duties as 'village missionary, tract distributor, and Sunday school promoter in a number of villages in Rutland and Northampton and in the Lincolnshire town of Stamford'— to quote his own words written later in his *Brief Notes on the Life, Labours, Sufferings and Death of Mrs. Marianne Cook*.

Leaving the Melbourne he loved was a wrench to Cook, and the monetary reward of his labours was scanty, a mere thirty-six pounds a year with perhaps a trifling commission on the tracts he sold. Nor was the evangelist always welcome. Though he was seldom subject to the brutal persecutions endured in the eighteenth century, yet there was always a possibility of ill-treatment from jeering and malicious toughs as one of the rigours of the job. Nevertheless its spiritual satisfactions must have seemed very real to a young man of his temperament, and there was much hospitality from the righteous to be enjoyed. But this enjoyment was tempered for, in 1829, 'on account of the great kindness of people among whom he laboured giving him so many presents, and, we judge, inviting him so frequently to their social board,' I quote the *Derby Reporter* of the eighteen-seventies—'they lowered

---

* Who succeeded Winks at Melbourne but subsequently emigrated to America.

his salary to £26 per annum.' But they could not reduce Cook's enjoyment of the countryside, when season and weather allowed. Travelling perforce was mostly done afoot, for the railways had not yet spread their network over the country. Though lifts from private vehicles might sometimes be had, public coaches or waggons could not be afforded on such funds as Cook's. In a diary for 1829, he records that he travelled 2,692 miles that year as a missionary, and that 2,106 of these were walked.

CHAPTER THREE

Romance and Abstinence

COOK was ever ready to tot up the miles covered in Good Work or Good Business to be presented at a later date to admiring audiences. He never said so: but it is clear that the sturdy mileage, done when his world was still young and innocent of railways, owed something to the heart as well as the head.

During the first year of his new work at Barrowden, in Rutland, he met Marianne Mason, a worker in the Baptist Sunday school and chapel. She had just turned one-and-twenty, was the daughter of a farmer and had five brothers. A younger sister having died in infancy, when her mother also died, the household cares of the farm had been shouldered by Marianne. She was young, fair at least in her lover's eyes, shared his intense religious convictions, and was capable and energetic. Thomas had no doubts. Blithe in his new-found happiness, he continued on his mission, preaching on village greens or in country chapels, selling or freely distributing from his pack the tracts, books, Bibles, and Testaments with which he was well laden.

Perhaps Marianne's menfolk had misgivings about the future of the couple? The young evangelist's salary precariously depended upon chance meagre funds. There could be little doubt of his capability. He was already showing a strength of character, integrity, a firmness of purpose, and a power of organizing his fellows. His aspect was that of a crusader for causes. It was a century in which the Common Man was taking religion into his own hands, but in which also righteousness was expected to march hand in hand with self-improvement. Industrial Britain was athrob with opportunity. If the right chance came his way, Marianne's earnest young suitor might do a great work in the world. But meanwhile? He had a trade. Might it not be better that he should work at that?

Events forced the issue. The Baptist churches were losing their zeal for home missions. Their funds were dwindling. It proved no longer possible for the Society which had sent him out to continue Thomas Cook as a paid agent. He therefore resigned his appointment and set himself up as a wood-turner and cabinet-maker in Barrowden, where, in view of his plans to marry, he soon found that there was insufficient scope for him. In the autumn of 1832, he accordingly moved to Market Harborough where, in the following spring, after a three-years' courtship, he married Marianne. His workshop was in Buzzard's Place. Their first home was at the Adam and Eve Street end of Quaker's Yard.

As if life were not varied enough with the first delights of marriage, the satisfaction of setting up a home, and the responsibility of establishing a business, Thomas Cook found time and energy enough not only to continue some evangelical work, albeit unpaid, but to become increasingly caught up in a new cause—that of temperance.

The eighteen-thirties saw the beginning of temperance agitation on a grand scale, a challenge to the increased drunkenness caused by the ill-advised Beerhouse Act of 1830. Eighteenth-century legislation had encouraged the distillation of spirits in England to counter the importation of foreign brandy. The consumption of cheap gin, particularly among the workers in the cities, was enormous.

Bad social conditions, of course, had as much to do with it as appetite. 'Drunk for a penny, dead drunk for twopence, clean straw for nothing' was the dram-shops' invitation to those in search of solace or oblivion. The excesses of the first half of the eighteenth century (portrayed with no exaggeration in Hogarth's *Gin Lane*) may have been checked by Acts of Parliament and by the influence of the Evangelical Revival, yet they continued to be alarming enough. Except among 'the People called Methodists' whose *Rules*, issued by the Wesleys in 1743, forbade the use of spiritous liquors, there was no formal opposition to the prevailing habits of the people. Then the government under Wellington, in its collective wisdom, decided that more beer would mean less spirits; and the Beerhouse Act was passed. This provided 'that any householder desirous of selling malt liquor, by retail, in any house, may obtain an excise licence on payment of two guineas, and for cider only, on paying one guinea.' Beyond this, only sureties were required for penalties incurred. Beerhouses might be open from 4 a.m. until 10 p.m., except during the hours of divine service on Sundays and holy days.

The results of establishing 'free trade' in beer were soon apparent. Even the poorest might keep a beerhouse, or let the beerhouse keep them, the more so when some brewers were willing to pay the two guineas for the licence and supply stock if the house were 'tied.' Thirty thousand new beerhouses were opened at once, and within six years of the passing of the Act, this number had increased to more than 44,000. Certainly, as the Act intended, more beer was drunk. But so, too, was more spirit. For the distillers met the competition of the beerhouses by building more flash gin-palaces whose glitter attracted custom to such purpose that the consumption of British-distilled spirits increased by a third during the decade of 1830-39.

Those who had favoured the measure were aghast.

THE SEMI-DETACHED COTTAGE AT MELBOURNE, DERBYSHIRE, WHERE THOMAS COOK WAS BORN

THE BERKELEY STREET HEADQUARTERS

Sydney Smith reported: 'The new Beer Bill has begun its operations. Everybody is drunk. Those who are not singing are sprawling. The sovereign people are beastly drunk.' Act after Act, over the years, attempted to cope with popular debauch by imposed legislative suppression. A more radical approach came from the pioneers of the early temperance movement, such as Joseph Livesey and his colleagues, from within the ranks of the people themselves. Their method of moral suasion aimed at social improvement by reformation of the individual who became a member of a local society on signing the pledge. They sought to permeate public opinion by meetings, demonstrations, and the publication and dissemination of tracts, pamphlets, and magazines. Most local societies were joined together in regional associations or were affiliated to national organizations who appointed local agents. When Thomas Cook settled in Market Harborough, the Rev. Francis Beardsall, the minister of the General Baptist Church at that place, was recognized as the agent of the British and Foreign Temperance Society. Beardsall preached temperance from his pulpit, and it was under his influence that, on New Year's Day, 1833, Cook signed the pledge: 'I agree to abstain from ardent spirits, and to discountenance the causes and practice of intemperance.' Mrs. Cook signed in the following May.

It was a pledge which only precluded the use of spirits, leaving other liquors to be used in strict moderation. Though not yet a professed total abstainer, Mrs. Cook would seem to have been so in practice, for it was his parents' later boast that their only son, John Mason, born at Market Harborough in January, 1844, had been a total abstainer from birth. The child was something of a phenomenon. For even most doctors, when almost everyone from their early days was used to intoxicating liquors of one kind or another, seem to have been uncertain about the possible physiological effects of abstinence. It was usual for nursing mothers 'to take something to keep up their strength' and querulous infants were so often quietened with a drop of gin that one of the many cant names for the spirit was Daffy's Elixir, after a well-known soothener. The progress of the little John Mason must have been watched with especial interest. As late as 1840, on the occasion of temperance junketings held at Windsor to celebrate Queen Victoria's marriage, we read that 'Among the "exhibitions" on the occasion was a fine infant of a Mr. Ford's, which is being suckled on the teetotal principle.'

By that date the stricter teetotal principle had indeed established itself. The organized total abstinence movement had taken its rise in Preston in 1832, with the famous signing of a pledge of abstinence 'from all liquors of an intoxicating quality' by seven working men led by Joseph Livesey. The influence of the 'Seven Men of Preston' spread outwards. It was at Preston also that the movement got its name, when, at a meeting in September, 1833, Dicky Turner, a reformed drunkard, emphasizing the need for entire abstinence, stuttered that "nothing but tee-tee-total will do.' Whereupon John Livesey cried out: 'That shall be the name.'

During 1834, the Rev. Francis Beardsall moved to Manchester, and there became a teetotaller. Early in the following year he visited Harborough and persuaded about a dozen people, including Mrs. Cook, but not her husband, to give total abstinence a twelve-months' trial. All, save two, lapsed into temperance. Interest seemed dormant if not dead when in December, 1836, John Hockings, 'the Birmingham Blacksmith,' delivered a tee-total lecture in the town. On the following morning, Thomas Cook and six others met to enrol themselves as members of a Teetotal Society of which Cook was appointed secretary.

Meanwhile his business of wood-turning and cabinet-making thrived. He employed assistants and took apprentices. One of these latter was his half-brother, Simeon

Smithard,* who was bound to Thomas after an earlier
employment in a lace factory. He and the others now
presented a problem to the new teetotaller who, on the
morrow of signing the teetotal pledge, was not sufficiently
settled in principle to desist from brewing a sack of malt,
still thinking it necessary for his workmen, who worked
hard and imagined that they could not do without their
beer. He and his wife, he reported in after years, 'had
many a struggle to contrive how to dismiss the last brewing
of beer from our table. At last Mrs. Cook nobly determined
that no more should be brought up from the cellar. Then
arose the question: "What shall we do with the barrels?"
one of which contained thirty-six gallons of strong ale, and
another sixty gallons of table beer. Knowing that her
brother, Mr. Mason, of Barrowden, who supplied the malt,
felt himself necessitated to supply drink to his house and
farm labourers, we sent the thirty-six-gallon barrel by a
carrier from Great Easton to its destination. I don't know
the manner in which it was transported, but that barrel
created a great sensation all the way down the valley of
the Welland. For sending it I was considered a fool, but
it was indeed a teetotal advocate all through its journey
of twenty-five miles. I cannot say it was not tapped on the
way, for the carrier told me that many desired to taste it.
We still had to decide what to do with the sixty-gallon
barrel, but that difficulty was solved by turning the barrel
out of the cellar and placing it over an open drain at the
bottom of the Quaker's Yard, where the tap was taken out
and the liquor freely ran into the drain. There was then
but one remaining relic of drink in our house and that
consisted of two or three bottles of Mrs. Cook's home-made
grape wine. This we never drank after our pledge was
taken, but it was found to be diminishing by degrees, and,
on watching the actions of an apprentice, I saw him at

* Simeon has his own minor place in the Cook story, in which, however,
I can find no trace of his brother James, except for Thomas Cook's statement
that he, like Simeon, died suddenly at the age of sixty.

midnight, through a single square of glass, regaling himself on the wine. We then cleared out all that was left of the temptation, and from that day to this not a barrel, or a bottle has entered our house for consumption by any member of the family.'

The workmen and apprentices, who customarily lived in, seemed to have submitted themselves to Cook's new ruling. There was, however, one exception. Already something of a drunkard, Simeon Smithard, demanded his table-beer and, being refused, broke his indentures and absconded. He ran away on a bitterly cold and snowy day in February. Cook, supposing that he had made towards Northampton, sent two men in pursuit. He afterwards learnt that they got no further than the *Dolphin,* just round the corner, where pursuers and pursued put in a night's hard drinking. Smithard afterwards made his way to Derby and there, said Cook, 'he continued his drinking career for some time.'

Cook eagerly flung himself into his many new tasks as Secretary of the Harborough Temperance Society. His own business may have suffered, but he was used to working long hours, and what matter if the Cause prospered? What a useful exercise this was, too, in the craft of organization which would one day bring him such good material reward. Meetings had to be organized and the visits of spell-binding speakers had to be arranged suddenly. He himself spoke often, and though he never prepared a speech, the fame of his eloquence began to spread. There were the bazaars, galas and demonstrations which were so dependent in their ardour on the great movements which were sweeping through the Midlands. There was the great mass of correspondence kept up with other Societies and individuals. Cook was regularly a delegate at conferences. In all this multifarious activity he was always helped and supported by Marianne, already busy enough about her own pursuits.

Temperance advocates, like pugilists, seem to have been

given to sobriquets, such as 'The Birmingham Blacksmith.'
In 1837, making his way to London, 'The Manchester
Carpenter' stopped at Market Harborough and suggested
giving a lecture on teetotalism. But he was 'so singular and
uncouth in manners and appearance' that Cook and his
fellows were afraid to allow him on the platform. One of
them tempered the refusal by giving him a dinner, after
which the 'Carpenter' called on Cook in his workshop
where a man was making plain deal tables. 'Mr. Cook,' he
said, 'you had better set me to make tables. I could make
half-a-dozen a day like that.' Mr. Cook thought, judging
by appearances, that his visitor might be more successfully
employed in making tables than in temperance advocacy.
Nevertheless, he kept silence. 'The Manchester Carpenter'
took up his bundle and went on his way. Eventually he
arrived in London and, after more success as a temperance
agent than his reception at Harborough would suggest, he
married to some little advantage. He was thus enabled to
found a temperance magazine which was followed by other
cheap periodicals for the working-classes. So began the
fortunes of a firm that still uses the surname of John
Cassell as its imprint.

In 1838, Cook was one of fifty delegates who met to
form the South Midland Temperance Association. As the
meeting was held at Harborough, it is likely that he was a
prime mover in the business. 'This organization . . . either
by affiliation or the friendly acceptance of its advocates,
(soon) embraced an immense number of towns and
villages. Its boundary line going eastward, included
Uppingham, Oakham, Stamford, Peterborough, Oundle,
Wandsford, Kings Cliffe, Weldon, Brigstock, Kettering,
Wellingborough, Northampton, Daventry, Guilsboro',
Long Buckby, Husbands Bosworth, Rugby, Leamington,
Warwick, Stratford-on-Avon, Coventry, Hinckley, Burton-
on-Trent, Loughborough, Leicester, and many other
places in the outer circle, and within that circle almost
every town and village of importance. The conduct of the

Association was the responsibility of delegates who met quarterly in one or other of the principal towns it covered. 'T. Cook (Harborough)' of course usually appears in the list of names, and he was characteristically active among the voluntary workers whose efforts aided those of the full-time paid agents. The employment of these latter, usually on a quarterly basis, was spasmodic and depended on the chance of available funds.

The lot of any temperance worker in those early days was not an easy one. Active opposition to the movement was organized by brewers, publicans and others, and gave fine opportunities to the rowdy element. Nor could the sympathy of the authorities be relied upon. Market Harborough was notorious as having one of the most discordant and riotous of anti-teetotal mobs. The temperance meetings, held in the town hall, were nearly always interrupted. On one occasion the meeting was thrown into total darkness when the gas supply-pipe was cut through. Leading teetotallers were mobbed in the streets and the windows of their houses broken. Thomas Cook came in for his share of these attentions. His house was attacked and brickbats were hurled through the windows. Once he was felled by the leg-bone of a horse, taken from a dump and thrown at him. Cook was no ninny. He struggled up, gave chase and overtook his assailant at the entrance to the *Talbot* yard. He took him before the magistrates and secured a conviction, a matter probably of little moment to the culprit as presumably his fine was paid, as in other instances, by the instigators of the outrage, the members of a convivial club known as 'The Tenth.'

'In the midst of this fire of persecution,' wrote Thomas Cook long afterwards, 'Mrs. Cook was induced, though very reluctant at first to engage in the business, to open her house for the accommodation of Temperance travellers who desired freedom from the drinking practices of licensed hotels.' Thus, adventitiously, began another of the many strands of experience to be woven together in the later career of Thomas Cook.

About this time, Cook got some advantage from his earlier experiences. His work as a village missionary, when his preaching had been reinforced by the distribution of tracts and pamphlets, had shown him the value of the printed word. His association with Winks, at Melbourne and Loughborough, had given him some knowledge of printing, publishing, and distribution. And now when, thanks to his energy, Market Harborough had become established as the centre of the South Midland Temperance Association's activities, who more suitable than Cook to take over the organization of a tract depot and the establishing of the periodicals which the Association needed for its work?

CHAPTER FOUR

Digression on Drink

L ET me now break the chronological pattern to summarize in his own words the attitude of the more mature and celebrated Thomas Cook of the eighteen-eighties towards Drink and Drinking. The pamphlet before me is an account of the *Temperance Jubilee Celebrations at Leicester and Market Harborough arranged and compiled by Thomas Cook,* 1886, in which he prints a paper on 'Facts and Incidents . . . written . . . in Confirmation of Medical and Scientific Opinion on the Non-necessity of Alcoholic Beverages in Health and Disease.' 'On these topics I have been enabled during the forty years of my public labours and travels to form very definite opinions, and I have frequently expressed them in connection with parties travelling under my personal arrangements . . .' Space will not permit me to do more than briefly quote.

ENGLAND. 'At home we understand well the bearings of the Temperance Question, and the subject of the properties of intoxicating drinks has been well discussed during the fifty years now under review, and it is very satisfactory to find that at home those who doubted or those who opposed altogether our advocacy fifty years ago have now, in great numbers, come over to our views and adopted our practice.'

SCOTLAND. 'We had always a difficulty in Scotland in

making hotel arrangements of a satisfactory character, and this was in great measure owing to the inveterate love of whisky which has been the drink and the curse of that country. In other lands wine, and especially "Vin Ordinaire" of the weaker kinds are resorted to with very great freedom, and with less danger of intoxication; whilst in Scotland the masses of the people were very much stupefied by whisky, and it was hard work all through the Highlands and the principal cities and towns of that country to convince them of the absolute safety and propriety of abstaining from all intoxicating drinks. Nevertheless, this was done to a very great extent, and I have abundant reasons to believe that the example I set before my travellers who accompanied me through those districts, and the example others had upon Hotel Proprietors, produced effects of a very beneficial character.'

IRELAND. 'At Killarney I had been attending a meeting of hotel keepers, convened at one of the hotels, to consider my proposals and how they should be dealt with. The proprietor of the house where we met was himself addicted to the use of whisky, and at the close of the meeting, when there had been a great deal of discussion as to the suggestions I made and the proposals I submitted, this old gentleman gave manifest signs of being under the influence of whisky, and his son-in-law, who was with me, was very disgusted to think that I should witness such a scene as was witnessed that evening. He apologized for the old man, and said that he was most genial in every respect except when under the influence of whisky.'

FRANCE. 'I consider that it is one of the evils of the French Hotel System that the provision is made in connection with the table d'hôte for each diner to have a certain amount of wine though of the weakest character, and this seemingly costing nothing in addition to the actual price of the hotel accommodation. I fear this has had an unhappy effect in causing people to take the wine-bottle who would not under other circumstances have resorted to it; and I have observed with very much pain and serious concern, that since that time there has been in Paris especially a tendency to resort to stronger potations, and where a glass of water, or a cup of coffee, or some other unintoxicating beverage supplies to satisfy the tastes and desires of visitors to the hotels, now there has grown up a sad system of spirit drinking, and especially that most pernicious of all drinks, "Absinthe," under the influence of which the Parisian physical strength as well as morality have been considerably undermined . . .'

SWITZERLAND. '. . . at the end of the second year of my visits to Switzerland, a meeting of Hotel Proprietors of the country was convened in Geneva for the purpose of considering the character of my arrangements, and for the purpose also of manifesting their thankfulness for the service which I had rendered them. At that meeting a banquet was given to me: I was placed alongside the Chairman of the meeting, and with my bottle of lemonade before me I was treated with as much respect as those who partook heavily of wine . . . There was on one occasion an instance which caused me very considerable pain. A gentleman who had figured in England as a temperance lecturer, and had attracted large audiences by his eloquence, was seated with his wife and three or four other ladies around a table in one of the hotels of Geneva, and I saw that there was an array of wine-bottles before them. As I approached the gentleman he said to me, "Mr. Cook, have you begun to take the wines of the country?" I replied by one expression, which closed the conversation, "No, sir; I am a teetotaller." I never again heard that this gentleman took the Temperance platform in England, and though he did maintain a considerable amount of popularity as a public lecturer, I perceived that he had, as I supposed, abandoned the great principles which he had formerly advocated. My brother, Simeon Smithard, who was with me on that occasion, was equally astonished with myself, and he also was satisfied that the way in which I

had replied to the gentleman was the only effective way of
rebuking his practice.'

ITALY. 'Wine drinking in Italy was then, as it was in
France and Switzerland, one of the prevailing torments of
the people, though it was thought that the common wines
of Italy were less potent than those of France and Switzerland, and I was sometimes grieved to see my parties when
they stopped at wayside refreshment rooms go into the bar
and purchase large quantities of common drinks, the merits
of which they were utterly unacquainted with. I had such
a strong feeling in reference to this, and the evils that were
already beginning to be manifested in the shape of
prevalent diarrhœa amongst some of the weaker of the
party, that I remonstrated with them, and said to them
on going to the rooms, "Gentlemen, do not invest your
money in diarrhœa.'

THE HOLY LAND. 'At Nazareth, also, it was a great
delight to be able to drink at the pure Fountain from which
the maidens of the city were accustomed to fill their vessels
and carry them for home consumption and other uses. On
the whole I had abundant reason to be satisfied that we
never need lack good water, and I never felt that there was
any necessity to resort to the wines of the country. In
visiting Hebron, I made enquiry as to the preparation of
syrups from the famous grapes grown there, and I had no
difficulty whatever in procuring a bottle of what is called
in Palestine "dibs,"—a thick syrup made from pure
grapes, and so preserved that I was enabled to bring it
home, and keep it without fermentation for a very long
time . . . A very small proportion indeed of the grapes
grown in Syria were manufactured into intoxicating drink,
and that drink as presented at Jerusalem was one of the
simplest of the class of intoxicants. I remember on one
occasion when the Rev. Newman Hall and other ministers
were with us, going through the country with our party,
consisting of between twenty and thirty travellers, with
more than a dozen teetotalers; and it was evident through-

out the whole journey that the teetotalers were the most exempt from little ailments, especially diarrhœa, and altogether there was a happy freedom from inconvenience of every kind arising from the drinks taken. I am quite sure that parties going to Palestine with the desire to carry out the principles of Temperance will have no difficulty in attaining that object.'

EGYPT. 'In Egypt it is a proverb with many that people get fat on Nile water. There is something in that statement, for the whole country, both as regards vegetation and natural life of every kind, owes its source and nourishment to the Nile. The Nile comes down in many cases a turbid and dirty stream of yellow water, caused by the sand banks and other matter thrown into it, but that water, filtered as it is in the principal hotels in Cairo, is of the purest and finest description, and I should not be at all surprised at the verification of the fact that the inhabitants of the country get fat on Nile water.'

AMERICA. 'There was always an abundant supply of good milk, of pure water, and of tea and coffee, which could be had to almost any extent. There was one occasion on which I felt some doubt in connection with the journey in the month of July to the Western States, but at every station refreshment room I found people rushing to large glasses which were set before them, resembling very much some of our wines, especially the sherry usually drunk at dinner tables in England. I was almost afraid that some declension had taken place in the habits of the people at these refreshment rooms, but I ventured to ask at last what it was that they drank so freely, and my informant replied "Cold Tea." I tried this same drink, and I found that nothing ever quenched thirst, or ever satisfied a thirsty appetite, so well as cold tea. It seemed to be almost a universal drink with Americans at wayside refreshment rooms, and I adopted it myself as very practicable and palatable. It has been always very satisfactory to find that in the great hotels in America there

was no obligation to take intoxicating drink at the tables;
it was indeed always considered a thing which, if had at
all, should be had outside the dining-rooms, and hence
the bar connected with the large hotels was frequently a
separate and distinct proprietary; but altogether the
drinking facilities were separate from those of the common
table. In private parties and families where I was sometimes accustomed to mingle, I found that strong drinks
were never introduced on the table. America was in that
sense far ahead of other countries in reference to their
drinking habits.'

How did Cook and that 'total abstainer from birth,' his
son, reconcile their teetotal conscience with a business
which was by no means confined to teetotallers, supported
by staff recruited from all over the world who could
hardly be expected to be total abstainers? In one of the
magnificent leather-bound volumes with marbled end-
papers, in which father and son presented detailed
information about their arrangements for the Nile, for
instance, they made no attempt at pretending that the
wealthy passengers on those luxury cruises would have to
go dry. Describing three vessels of the Nile flotilla, 'so
generally popular that they have been engaged by private
families and many persons of distinction every season
since 1889,' this lush blurb states that there are no extras
to be paid, 'but that for wine, spirits and mineral waters.'
Of the 'Improved Saloon Passenger Steamers' it is said
that every one 'carries . . . a liberally-maintained cellar
of wines . . .'

Are we then submitting to humbug in paying such
attention to the strivings of our champion against the
demon drink, when ultimately he acquiesced and indeed
toadied to that suppressed frenzy of opulence, indulgence
and self-esteem with which the later Victorian British
regarded an Imperial world? Upon certain of the Nile
flotilla, there was 'a piano on the main deck, and concerts,
dances, and entertainments are encouraged and made

possible by closing in the whole upper deck at nightfall with canvas curtains.' Yet in the rules laid down by Cook for the Mission Hall at Melbourne, it was stated that it was not to be 'let for dramatic entertainments, or for dancing or any amusements of like kind.'

I prefer to console myself with the thought that such apparent inconsistencies are not so much humbug as an expedient liberalism which was typical of those go-getting times.

Thomas Cook explained, with some nicety, how in Egypt his firm 'resolved to "keep our hands clean from this contamination." ' It was simply a matter of foisting it upon other consciences than their own. 'Wherever drinks were required, it was a matter of simple arrangement between the Dragoman or the refreshment contractor and the traveller.' Toward his own pensioners at Melbourne, he was much more strict. Toward his employees as they multiplied, he could only stress his principles up to a point. Old employees who began their service in frock coats tell me that Cook or his son always insisted that for any work they did on Sundays, the ungodly reward should go into their pockets and not his own. When civilization created the expense sheet, that now-potent familiar companion of so many modern travellers, it was never to be tainted by any item of alcohol, though buckets of mineral water would be admitted. Most of the former frock-coated ones, honest men of the world all, agree that it was better to wear the blue ribbon of abstinence when seeking a job.

I need hardly add that the present organization does not look for teetotalism as a serious qualification for the ten thousand people it employs. Nor is abstinence included in the curriculum of the staff-training courses which run from four to eight weeks and cover the mass of facts, the sense of geography and the professional manner which go to make up a Man-From-Cooks.

CHAPTER FIVE

The Crusader

Both Cook and his son remained faithful to the Harborough pledges; and the wider issues of alcoholism or an international staff management were not present to tax the ardent integrity of the young couple whose concern was the South Midland Depository, also styled Temperance Depot, which was widely advertised as being situated in Adam and Eve Street, and may therefore almost certainly be taken as being housed under their own roof. The Depository was opened early in 1839 as a centre for the sale and distribution of temperance publications (tracts, pamphlets and periodicals), pledge cards and medals, for the convenience of societies within the Association. Subscriptions were solicited in order that sales might be at the lowest possible rates. Financial responsibility belonged to the Association. Cook's time and trouble were rewarded by a commission on sales which the available data suggests as ten per cent. The venture was never capitalized, however, and as business increased, Cook found its conduct increasingly difficult. After two years, in February, 1841, he protested to his fellow delegates that 'something *must be done*, and done *soon*, or myself, and your printer, will be sufferers to a serious extent.' Six of the delegates thereupon advanced £5 each against the proceeds of future bazaars, but in

April, 1841, it was agreed that 'a Committee be appointed to make arrangements with Mr. Cook, for the future management of the Tract Depot, in order that all responsibility may be taken from the Association, and that Mr. Cook carry it on, in future, on his own responsibility.'

By this time, Cook was engaged at the Depot not only as a wholesale and retail distributor of tracts and the rest, but also as a publisher. He was also editor and publisher of two monthly periodicals and other temperance ephemera. The earliest by a little of these periodicals was the official organ of the South Midland Temperance Association. The first number of *The Monthly Temperance Messenger* was issued at a penny in November, 1839. The February 1840 issue, enlarged, announced itself proudly at 'No. 1, Vol. 1' of the 'New Series' of *The Temperance Messenger and Tract Magazine*, which contrived a precarious existence until the end of a fifth volume in 1844. The unillustrated contents were of necessity somewhat stereotyped: a few general articles or reports of lectures were supported by news of Association activities, there were brief notices of temperance publications and, as fill-ups, anecdotes—but what masterpieces of uplift were to be found among these. My own favourite, perhaps because of a fondness for the ballad *'Please sell no more drink to my father'*, which I first heard revived by Miss Elsa Lanchester between the wars, is headed *Hardening Influence of the Traffic*. I cannot resist quoting it in full. 'In one of the quiet towns of Massachusetts, a young lady, the only child of her parents, who had an accomplished education, and all the charms of modest beauty and noble intellect, went to a rum-seller who was daily enticing her father to drink, intending soon to possess his snug little farm. She told him he was not only destroying her father, but bringing ruin and disgrace upon her and her mother. O, he said, she would soon be married, she need not trouble herself. She replied, she never would—she could never consent to involve in their shame one that she loved—she would

never leave her mother, but would work with her own
hands, and every day bring him the amount of money
he now received from her father, if he would sell
him no more. She entreated him with tears. But, with
an infernal leer, he asked the poor girl if he should say
to her *father* that she had *requested* him to sell him no
more. Her eye flashed—and reason reeled. "*You are not
a man!*" said she. She is now a maniac in the Worcester
Asylum!'

The sixteen small pages were usually enclosed in a
wrapper which bore advertisements and so produced a
little revenue. Circulation, at its peak, does not seem
to have exceeded 1,500 copies, and it was a constant
plaint that 'the *Messenger* hardly covers expenses' even
though the editors laboured 'gratuitously for the good
of the Cause.' Cook seems to have shared the editorship at the outset. Later, as we shall see, he assumed sole
responsibility.

From its start, in January, 1840, Thomas Cook, however, was the only editor of *The Children's Temperance
Magazine, A Cabinet of Instruction and Amusement for Little
Teetotallers, edited by a Father.* Cook thus founded the
first children's temperance magazine to be published in
England. It appeared as a penny monthly and juvenile
appetite was whetted by the promise of 'at least four cuts.'
It was most probably similar in size to the *Messenger*, as
bound volumes of either could be had at eighteenpence
each. It ran for seven or eight years. No copies are in the
British Museum Library, nor have I been able to trace
any elsewhere. As with other later Cook publications, its
ephemeral nature, small circulation, and mainly local
appeal minimized any chance of survival. Copies were
already scarce nearly seventy years ago. Thomas Cook
himself was advertising for a run of *The Children's Temperance Magazine,* and other items, in 1886. Since then, the
ravages of time and salvage have made any survival
extremely unlikely.

A correspondent of the magazine directed his envelope as follows:

'The person to whom this letter should go
Lives in Adam and Eve Street, Market Harbro':
He neither drinks Ale, nor Brandy nor Wine,
Nor anything else on the Publican's sign;
He edits a book on the Teetotal plan,
And tries to reform the world if he can;
But lest you should not find him out by his book,
He is a Wood Turner, and named THOMAS COOK.'

The last line may serve to remind us that Thomas Cook was still engaged in his ordinary business as wood-turner and cabinet-maker. I am inclined to think that his other activities must have conflicted with the interests of his livelihood. His temperance advocacy was voluntary, his editorial work was unpaid, and the business of the tract depository can only have brought him a few pounds a year. His statement that, in 1840, 'near' 100,000 tracts were published and 100,000 more, from other sources, were distributed, sounds impressive. But the usual price of four-page tracts was then sixteenpence a hundred, and you may hazard your arithmetic. At all events, a correspondent of the *Harborough Advertiser* in 1941 recalled that about 1841 Cook 'was apparently hard up, and he came to my mother and asked her to give him some work. My mother said, "You can make me a music stool!" ' This correspondent, Mr. E. A. Goward, added, 'That relic, a four-legged music stool, is now (June 30th, 1941) in my possession.' One cannot but suppose that Thomas Cook had a standard at least of sound craftsmanship, and many pieces from his workshop must still usefully survive in the Market Harborough neighbourhood. It has been suggested that the bookcases which he presented to the Baptist Sunday schools at Melbourne, Barton and Market Harborough in 1889 were of his own making as well as design. I think this is improbable. He was then upwards of eighty years old, failing in sight and general health.

The music stool incident happened just about the time that inspiration and practical common sense were to fuse and create that career by which the world knows of Thomas Cook. Henceforth, music stools were to be of dwindling moment to him. The steam revolution, though he was hardly aware of it, had come about during the years of his early manhood. The Midland roads, so familiar to him within the limited range of his journeyings, were being superseded by railways.

Hitherto only the well-to-do had been able to afford their own or hired carriages. Journeys by stage-coach were hazardous, uncomfortable, expensive and slow; and not much less so by the mail. Most working people, and indeed many others, had never travelled far from their birthplaces unless, like Cook, they had employed 'Shanks' naggie.' Although locomotives had been used in mines before Cook was born, their possible use in drawing passenger traffic was for long considered a visionary notion. As late as 1829, the Duke of Wellington satisfied himself that there was no reason for supposing that the steam-carriage would 'force itself into general use.' Yet, in the previous year, George Stephenson's *Rocket*, on trial, had done twenty-eight to twenty-nine miles an hour, a speed four times that of the average coach. A year later, the Duke himself was present at the opening of the Liverpool and Manchester railway, when he saw his friend William Huskisson, Member for Liverpool, killed as he stepped in front of an engine which was unprovided with a brake. Incidentally, a descendant, Mr. Edward Huskisson, was general manager of the firm of Thos. Cook & Son from 1935 until his retirement in May, 1947.

The Liverpool-Manchester, which opened in 1830, was the first line regularly to engage in passenger traffic, although its promoters built it primarily for the conveyance of goods. During its first year it carried no fewer than

445,000 people. A train of average length could carry as many passengers as thirty mail-coaches, as many goods as a hundred coaches, and either at much cheaper rates. Despite prejudice and opposition, the railway age was at hand. During the next few years, scores of small local lines were built throughout the country. Later, after the collapse of the railway boom of the early '40's, many were amalgamated in one or other of the greater systems. 'Bradshaw's Railway Guide showed two hundred railways in 1846, but in 1848 only twenty-two large and a few small ones.'

Almost eleven years after the opening of the Liverpool-Manchester line, in the early summer of 1841, Thomas Cook, at the age of thirty-three, had only once made a journey by rail. Unaware of the significance of the threshold he was crossing, he set out from Harborough on June 9th of that year to attend a temperance meeting by walking the fifteen miles to Leicester.

CHAPTER SIX

The Glorious Thing

THOMAS COOK liked to tell his own story. Let's listen to his account of the momentous occasion:

'I believe that the Midland Railway from Derby to Rugby *via* Leicester was opened in 1840. . . . The reports in the papers of the opening of the new line created astonishment in Leicestershire, and I had read of an interchange of visits between the Leicester and Nottingham mechanics institutes. . . . About midway between Harborough and Leicester—my mind's eye has often reverted to the spot—a thought flashed through my brain—what a glorious thing it would be if the newly-developed powers of railways and locomotion could be made subservient to the promotion of temperance! That thought grew upon me as I travelled over the last six or eight miles. I carried it up to the platform, and strong in the confidence of the sympathy of the Chairman, I broached the idea of engaging a special train to carry the friends of temperance from Leicester to Loughborough and back, to attend a quarterly delegate meeting appointed to be held there in two or three weeks following. The Chairman approved, the meeting roared with excitement, and early next day I proposed my grand scheme (which included, Cook forgets to mention here, 'an attraction in the shape of a Gala') to John Fox Bell, the resident secretary of the Midland Counties Railway.'

'I know nothing of you or your society,' Cook was told, 'but you shall have the train.' And, moreover, Bell handed him a contribution towards the preliminary expenses.

The following week or two must have been a busy and anxious time for Cook. Arrangements had to be made at Loughborough for the gala and for feeding the anticipated crowds. Invitations were sent to Nottingham, Derby and other places, whence supporters duly arrived, two 'special carriages' from Derby alone bringing 'about one hundred friends.' The event had to be publicized and tickets not only printed but sold. The reduced third-class fare for 'Mr. Thos. Cook's Excn. Leicester to Loughborough and back,' a distance of eleven miles, was a shilling.

At last came Monday, July 5th, 1841. Five hundred and seventy people crowded on to the platform at the Leicester station preceded by the band which was to accompany them and the sightseers who were not. Somehow they were got into the nine open carriages or 'tubs,' provided for them. These were of the usual third-class accommodation of the period—seatless open trucks in which the passengers stood unsheltered from the weather and liable to all hazards.

When the 'near six hundred men and women all going ahead per Railway, to crush the monster Intemperance' were met by Leicester crowds, a procession was formed which, headed by the band, marched through the town to the park where their demonstration was to be held. 'As the procession passed the Barracks, a singular scene was presented; a number of dragoons got astride the roof of the building, and being stripped to their shirts and wide white trousers, their fine proportions appeared swelled to those of Patagonians. The windows were also crowded with fierce moustachioed faces, one of which, in particular, attracted our attention. This soldier, like those on the roof, was stripped, his head was clothed with a queer red woollen nightcap, his moustachios were large and black, and he regarded the moving, joyful crowd beneath him with the imperturbable gravity of a Turk.'

The procession was temporarily dismissed at Mr. Paget's park where its members made short work of the hams and loaves which Cook had provided for them. Then it re-formed, went to meet contingents from Derby, Nottingham and Harborough, and, swollen by these, made an afternoon progress through the Loughborough streets. Nearly a thousand teetotallers and Rechabites, old 'reformed drunkards' with young 'teetotallers from birth,' all proud in their bravery of ribbons, medals and rosettes, some carrying white wands, others helping to bear aloft the silk and satin flags and banners which flaunted their purple, blue, white and red, all excited to be marching to the brassy blare of the Leicester band.

The fortunate got tea. Cook had catered for a thousand and as many more had turned out to support the pledged teetotallers. The band indefatigably played in the centre of the park. Some danced, others played cricket. There were games of 'drop handkerchief' and such innocent sports. From six o'clock on, for three hours, speeches were made from a rigged-up wagon-platform. Afterwards, there was the business of getting home. The Leicester train, Cook's main concern, arrived at half-past ten. It was nearly dark, but a great crowd had gathered to welcome home the intrepid teetotallers who were treated as pioneers who had performed a notable feat. Cook had reason to be proud of the event. Not least because his excursionists had all returned 'in perfect safety, not the slightest accident having occurred during the day,' but I think also because he had discovered that a man of the people like himself could so readily influence the seemingly infinite powers of steam.

That day's events certainly founded the fortunes of Thos. Cook & Son; but one must be wary of more extravagant claims. Cook's first excursion has sometimes been described as the earliest of all railway excursions. This is not true; and Cook himself, though not averse to recounting the story of the day, never made that claim, although he did affirm 'that I had the honour of conducting the first public Excursion Train ever known in England.'

There were, of course, excursions before that first one of his. Some of these, though not all, were for the benefit of organizations and, being presumably restricted to their members, were not considered as public. Cook himself, in articles in *The Leisure Hour*, refers to the two exchange excursions by the Nottingham and Leicester Mechanics' Institutes, both in July, 1840, run at half the normal fares. Even, though he was unaware of it, while Cook was making his arrangements for the Leicester to Loughborough trip, the Committee of the Birmingham Mechanics' Institute announced, in the *Birmingham Journal*, June 12th, 1841, that an excursion of their members would take place by rail to Cheltenham and Gloucester on June 29th.

Thus another claim would fail, that Cook's was the first publicly-advertised excursion, even if there were not yet earlier instances. A correspondent of the *Birmingham Post*, July 8th, 1891, referred to an excursion from Birmingham to York, at a return fare of three-and-sixpence, as taking place 'just before or just after 1840,' and being 'advertised all round the district.' This is somewhat vague, but when, in August, 1838, special trains were run on the Whitby and Pickering line for the benefit of a bazaar in aid of a church building fund, the posters announced: *The train will leave at five o'clock in the morning, and parties will have to be wide awake at an early hour, or they will suffer disappointment. Promptitude on the part of the railway calls for the same from the passengers.* No copy, alas, survives of any poster announcing the earliest 'special' traced in connection with a public event. This was for a public execution at Bodmin, in 1838. Two brothers, named Lightfoot, had been sentenced to death for the murder of a Wadebridge business man. The Wadebridge folk were eager to exact their vicarious revenge and in the early morning of the 'turning off' a special train was run down the line between the two places. The 'arrangements' would have done credit to a Cook. The gallows were in full sight of the uncovered station, and it was unnecessary for the passengers to leave the open railway carriages.

If then, by the time of Cook's first excursion venture, there had been other excursions, both public and private and of necessity advertised, how did these compare in point of scale and of arrangements? We have seen that Cook provided refreshments for his excursionists, but we do not know whether payment for these was included in the fare-charge, though this would seem unlikely. But in June, 1840, an excursion to York, over the Leeds and Selby and the York and North Midlands Railways, had been organized for the members of the Leeds Mechanics' Institute, when fares at half the normal rates had included for tea at York, this being the earliest-known instance of such all-in arrangements. Then, while Cook's waybill of 570 passengers is considerable, it cannot compare with the 1,250 carried in 40 carriages, the largest number until then ever linked together in one train, on one of the earliest Sunday excursions from Leeds to Hull, also in 1841.

It is thus possible to demolish various claims that have been casually made for Cook's first excursion, though not, I hasten to add, by the firm of Thos. Cook & Son, whose attitude in the matter is one of admirable caution. Perhaps his own phrase 'conducting the first public Excursion Train' was unintentionally somewhat ambiguous and should be recast to read that he was the first to conduct a public excursion train in England. For there remains the question of 'personally conducting' an excursion. And here, I think, Cook's reputation as a pioneer may stand. For it is obvious that, on such excursions as those organized by Mechanics' Institutes, and others on behalf of the employees of industrial concerns, some one or other on the train must have been accepted by his fellows as being in responsible charge, yet these excursions were not public. Certainly the railway employees had their responsibilities on all trains, excursion or otherwise, public or private. But it must be remembered that, in the early days of steam travel, both railway servants and public were inexperienced and accidents were not uncommon. Thomas Cook always stressed the importance of his excursions being personally conducted, and there is no doubt that this was an integral factor of his success. Many of his passengers must have been travelling by rail for their first time. The exuberance of some had to be checked, the timidity of others reassured, the comfort and safety of all to be looked after. The vicar of East Dereham, Norfolk, the Rev. Benjamin Armstrong, an excursionist fourteen years on, gives us a glimpse of Cook on a railway platform: 'Mr. Cook . . . was a great man to-day. Crowds obeyed his instructions implicitly and certainly regarded him as an infallible authority. Frantic and agitated females such as are always to be seen on railway platforms, even these obey Mr. Cook, and their minds are at peace.'* It was in a great measure owing to this control that Cook could subsequently claim that 'to my knowledge, not a single accident has happened to one of my Excursion Trains by which life or limb has been impaired.'

Nevertheless, when he went to bed, no doubt late and exhausted, upon that July night in 1841, the fervent little teetotaller could not have foreseen how far he would travel along rails. John Ruskin, his near contemporary, was to write, 'Going by railroad I do not consider as travelling at all; it is merely being "sent" to a place, and very little different from becoming a parcel.' To that parcelling which the æsthete found so unedifying, the still obscure Midland moralist had a tremendous contribution to make. For the moment, the new travel was exciting to most, perplexing to many and a high adventure to those earnest souls who sought to 'crush the monster Intemperance,' and

* *A Norfolk Diary*, Ed. Herbert B. J. Armstrong (Harrap), 1949, p. 38.

to whom even their capital city lay beyond the remotest horizon.

It is unlikely, all the same, that Cook went to bed that night realizing that he had done anything out of the ordinary. He had undertaken to organize an excursion in the cause of temperance. He had done so. He had travelled, as a matter of course, with the excursionists. Naturally he had exerted himself on their behalf. Admittedly it had been a success. But he might have deprecated that the success was mainly due to his own force of personality, strength of character and talent for organization.

It is not surprising that he was asked to arrange other excursions. During the remainder of that first summer and throughout the summer months of 1842-44, he was kept so increasingly busy in arranging and conducting excursions for temperance society members and for Sunday school children that, in the last of these summers, he found nearly all his time taken up by what he was later to call these 'amateur performances.'

The amateur performances, depending on the co-operation of the Midland Counties Railway and the extent of that system, at first only linked Leicester, Nottingham, Derby and Birmingham, but were afterwards extended from Derby to Rugby, while beauty spots such as Matlock and Mount Sorrel were also visited. The popular rate for all the excursions was a shilling for adults and sixpence for children. These minimum fares covered even the hundred miles' run from Derby to Rugby and back, or the longer trip still from Leicester to Birmingham by way of Derby.

Perhaps the most 'Cookian' of these early ventures was the trip arranged, in September, 1843, from Leicester to Derby, in order to snatch the Sunday school children of Leicester out of temptation's way at the time of the races. 'I proposed to the Leicester Sunday school teachers to take their schools to Derby, and all the teachers of that town to open their schoolrooms and provide tea for those of the same religious denominations. The proposal was responded to at both ends of the line. On the first day, 3,000 children were conveyed in every kind of vehicle that could be mustered, including a number of new, never-before-used iron coal wagons. The ordinary rolling-stock was inadequate to the occasion; and, with the wagon supplements filled to their utmost capacity, we still left behind 1,500 little enthusiasts for a second day.'

CHAPTER SEVEN

Printer and Publisher

WHAT, meanwhile, was happening to the Good
Works? It will be remembered that, in April,
1841, the delegates of the South Midland Temperance Association agreed to relinquish to Cook the
tract depository at Market Harborough. They were making
a virtue of almost necessity. For though the concern had
limped along without capital, and receipts just covered
outgoings, it was difficult to continue to work, much less
to develop it, without adequate finance. Yet it must
somehow be continued. If the Association could not, then
Cook would shoulder the responsibility. The depository to
him was the core of the Association's activities. 'The thirst
for information increases,' he maintained; 'and if it be
desirable to publish Temperance works, it is equally
desirable to have the best machinery for getting them into
circulation.'

Perhaps he was already contemplating the move he was
to make towards the end of the year. His zeal for the
temperance cause having perhaps jeopardized his livelihood from the wood-turning business, he may well have
decided that his drive and energy in a busier centre than
Market Harborough would better provide for his wife and
small son, if he were to engage in the full-time business of
printing as well as publishing and distributing temperance

publications. In June he was offering the old stock of the South Midland depository at a reduction of fifty per cent. In the same month a project was published for 'the erection of a splendid and commodious Temperance Hall at Leicester' in which, although its performance was to be delayed for almost ten years, it is not difficult to see the hand of Cook. *The Temperance Messenger* had previously been printed by Phillips of Northampton, and 'A. Cockshaw, Leicester,' is a usual imprint on the Association tracts. In the October issue of the *Messenger*, however, we read that at a delegates' meeting in the previous month 'An arrangement was made for printing it after the present year.' Consequently, in November, 1841, Thomas Cook removed to Leicester, and set up the Midland Temperance Press at 1 King Street, an address soon altered to 26 Granby Street, where Mrs. Cook, fortified by her experience of putting up temperance visitors in her home at Market Harborough, opened a temperance hotel.

By this time the young John Mason Cook—the Augustus Cæsar of *The Times* leader—begins to assume a regular place in the Cook story. His parents could not afford him more than an elementary education. He was first sent to a dame's school and then to a British school at Market Harborough. A disposition to organized travel showed itself when he was remarkably young: 'When six years old he made a trip from Market Harborough to Melbourne in Derbyshire, his father's birthplace. The first day he walked from Harborough to Kibworth, the second he went by omnibus from Kibworth to Leicester, the third he went by rail from West Bridge to Long-lane, thence by canal boat to Shardlow, and from Shardlow to Derby by omnibus. On the fourth day he was carried to Melbourne from Derby by Green's carrier's van.'*

The little Cook was early pressed into active teetotal

* *The Business of Travel: A Fifty Years Record of Progress.* W. Fraser Rae, 1891, p.222. A jubilee publication, this book is a useful guide to the history of the first fifty years of Thos. Cook & Son. It should, however, be used circumspectly in matters of detail, especially in the earlier chapters.

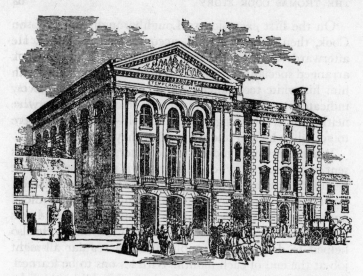

THE TEMPERANCE HALL AND THE TEMPERANCE HOTEL, GRANBY STREET, LEICESTER. FLANKED BY THE 'NAG'S HEAD,' ON THE LEFT, AND THE 'WAGGON AND HORSES' ON THE RIGHT.

service. More than fifty years later he was to recall an incident at this time: 'I remember once preparing, or being prepared, to make a speech. I was drilled by one of the best of grandmothers into an address. She wrote it for me; she taught me to render it; she rehearsed me on several chairs, and she decided that I delivered that speech admirably—to her perfect satisfaction. I had learned every word of it, but when I arrived at the building in Derby at which I was to deliver it (I was then so small that they had to place me on a chair), I got as far as "Ladies and Gentlemen" (although they were only very young ladies and gentlemen present, like myself). I repeated that three or four times, and that was all I could remember of the speech, of which I knew every word before I entered the room. A friend of mine got up and said that their young friend from Market Harborough was evidently not prepared to address them; and therefore they would excuse him.'

On the first excursion to Loughborough, John Mason Cook, then seven years old, accompanied his father. He afterwards went on the excursions which Thomas Cook arranged specially for Sunday school children, taking with him his white teetotaller's wand 'with which he gravely indicated to his fellow-passengers—most of whom were neither older nor bigger than himself—where they were to go, while he also told them what they were to do.'

When the Cooks moved to Leicester, John Mason was sent to a preparatory school there. It is not surprising that he failed to get much benefit from his part-time attendance. For the fees were more than his parents could well afford and, in order that he might earn something, the lad was put to learn 'the case' in his father's printing office. He also helped to despatch the publications, a regular all-night job at the end of each month. With lessons to be learned, the craft of printing and the job of publishing to be mastered, excursions in their season to be conducted and temperance meetings at all seasons always to be attended, Satan can have found little mischief for John Mason's hands.

We get a glimpse of him, soon after his tenth birthday, in the at-first surprising company of Simeon Smithard, Thomas Cook's half-brother, whom we left steering a drunken course for Derby after he had broken his indentures to Cook at Market Harborough. Smithard drank himself sick and sorry at Derby and, under the care of his mother, was converted and became a member of the Baptist Church. He signed the pledge and returned to Cook at Harborough, a 'reformed drunkard,' to be instructed as a temperance advocate. As such, he enjoyed great popularity, 'especially for his singing of choice temperance songs and melodies.' Smithard was appointed an agent to the South Midland Temperance Association and it is in a report of his that we read of him accompanied by John Mason Cook: 'Went to Belgrave, in company with Master John Cook, a teetotaller from his birth, of ten

THE OLD HEADQUARTERS AT LUDGATE CIRCUS

THE COOK NILE STEAMERS WERE BUILT MORE FOR COMFORT THAN SPEED

years' standing. We distributed tracts from house to house, and invited the people to a meeting on the green in the evening. We commenced the meeting at 7 o'clock, and not a little interest was excited by the calm and deliberate manner of my young companion in opening the meeting by giving out "let temperance and her sons rejoice. . . ." '

For Thomas Cook, the early eighteen-forties were years of endeavour to establish his new business with but modest financial reward, though much toil. He not only edited and published but also printed *The Temperance Messenger*, which however remained the organ and property of the South Midland Temperance Association. He continued to edit and produce *The Children's Temperance Magazine*. In May, 1842, he launched another, twelve-page, penny monthly, *The Anti-Smoker and Progressive Temperance Reformer*. In the previous March and April issues of the *Messenger* he had inveighed against 'the lovers of the filthy atmosphere of smokeries.' Association members who smoked complained to the delegates and he had been requested to keep, for the time being, an editorial silence on this topic. He loyally agreed, as far as the *Messenger* was concerned. But his effective retort to his critics was 'the first periodical organ of anti-tobaccoism the world ever knew.' It denounced 'the use of tobacco, snuff, cigars, and opium, with all other intoxicating agents—solid, liquid, or fluid.'

Cook himself would seem by now to have been holding up the general idea of temperance as an umbrella over a number of very vaguely connected causes. 'An impression has gone abroad that the editor of this periodical is a meddlesome sort of person, who is trying to "mix up other subjects" with Teetotalism,' he defensively complains in an early number. It should be admitted that he aided that impression. 'We rejoice to be of the number . . . who are opposed to *all war*,' he had previously written, and later glossed this with, 'I am a man of peace, and a member of the Peace Society.' He found room for a discussion on

C

hydropathy, or the cold-water cure, then in great vogue. He attacked patent medicines, coming out particularly and strongly against the 'quackery' and 'humbugging' of Wesley's Family Pills, thereby drawing the fire of the proprietors of that panacea. His wish, indeed, was to aid every attempt to propagate just views and enforce right practices respecting meats and drinks, habits and customs, adding that 'our *Reformer* is but a little child, and though possessed of (we hope) a large soul, more topics cannot well be embraced at present.' In this respect it was a period, not unlike our own, of affecting infant mortality. With other 'little children,' the *Reformer* found its efforts to survive too much for a defective circulation. Lack of capital and the stress of the 'sale or return' system further helped to bring on the end in December, 1843.

An interesting glimpse of Thomas Cook at this time, in his mid-thirties, is self-given in the last, third, volume of *The Anti-Smoker*. In *Scraps from the Note Book of a Tourist*, announced too optimistically as 'to be continued,' Cook describes how he 'left home for the purpose of a week's excursion among the teetotallers of the Peak of Derbyshire and parts of Yorkshire. . . . My desire was to breathe uncontaminated air, and this wish, combined with a principle of economy, led me to take a "tub" ticket at the station. All railway travellers know that smoking is strictly prohibited in all the railway carriages; but it is also well known that this law is often violated. Thus it was on the above morning. At the Syston station (the first from Leicester) two young men got into the carriage and placed themselves just before me on the opposite seat. I soon discovered that they had something in their hands which they attempted to hide from the view of the police. As soon as the train started, a box of lucifers was produced, a light struck, and one of the men placed a cigar between his lips, and the other a short black pipe . . . the current of wind carrying the smoke directly in my face. I endured the nuisance as patiently and as silently as possible until a young gentleman of Leicester, who knew my anti-smoking propensities, whispered in my ear: "Where are your principles?" I replied that I was pondering in my breast whether I should lay an information at the next station, or talk to them. It occurred to me that I had under the seat a parcel containing a quantity of the Tract—*Friendly Advice on the Use of Tobacco*. I opened the parcel and drew out one of the tracts, which I placed in the hand of the young man who sat nearest to me. I simply asked him to read. He read the title and turned it to the next page, after reading a few lines of which he hastily took his pipe from his mouth and flung it away . . . after reading a few pages further, he drew from his waistcoat pocket a paper containing his stock of tobacco, which he vehemently cast away, declaring that he had "done with that," and, turning to his companion said, "Come, down with that cigar— and the snuff-box must go too . . ."

'This pleasing instance of the powerful operations of simple truth, administered in a kind manner, was particularly gratifying and encouraging. I thought how much better it was that I had adopted the course I took than it would have been to have dictated the laying of an information against my fellow passengers. In that case I might have expected a manifestation of revengeful feelings, for they had the appearance of uncouth labouring men. . . . I also resolved that in future I would always arm myself with a supply of anti-tobacco ammunition when I have to travel by rail . . .'

Although *The Anti-Smoker* died, *The Children's Temperance Magazine* continued to find support until 1847 or 1848, but *The Temperance Messenger* only lingered on until the end of 1844.

Before this, the undaunted Cook had begun to issue a more ambitious monthly, *The National Temperance Magazine*, a sixpenny affair of forty pages, which seems to have lasted until mid-1846, and which he somewhat unblushingly announced as the development of the *Anti-Smoker*.

About 1844 he also 'took over from the late Mr. John Waddington not only his leading printer, Mr. W. Durrad, but also the *Youth's Biblical Cabinet*, which I edited for a twelve month.' What prodigious energies went into these years of Good Works before he became a professional travel man. Besides editing, printing and publishing his temperance tracts and periodicals and much else, and being engaged in the general business of a printer, he found time, continuing of course his Baptist interests, to work generally for the South Midland Temperance Association as Secretary, to attend various conferences as a delegate, to support such other causes as warrant his own self-description as a progressive temperance reformer, and to arrange—and conduct—as an amateur—temperance and other excursions. As corresponding secretary of the Leicester Temperance Society, he took a leading part in its activities, regularly speaking at the Monday weekly meetings and working in the Sunday school for youths and adults.

Cook's temperance publications, other than periodicals, issued from the Midland Temperance Press, included a number of tracts. He often stated later that, at this period, he had issued 'at least half a million tracts on Temperance and kindred subjects.' This seems a great many, though in point of fact his usual runs were about 2,000 copies, and it therefore works out at 250 titles spread over a number of years, a total again lessened by the fact that some tracts went into more than one edition. Many of the tracts were issued in series, such as *The Teetotaller's Pocket Library*. They are thirsty reading.

Cook's temperance almanacks were probably the most successful of the Midland Temperance Press ephemera. He had projected the first of these 'on a much larger scale than any yet,' in August, 1841, and had appealed for information and advertising support against a printing of 5,000 copies in the September issue of the *Messenger*. The resulting *National Temperance Almanack for* 1842 was,

according to Dawson Burns,* published at sixpence, a
price which was halved for its successor of the following
year, characterized by the same authority as 'probably
the best of its kind which had hitherto appeared in
England.' The contents of both issues were presumably
much the same. Cook had advertised his intention to
supply in the first place a complete list of the temperance
hotels in the kingdom; information as to district associations, their halls, periodicals and other publications;
temperance statistics; and short original papers. In 1842
Cook also published *The National Temperance Almanack for*
1843, which in December he was able to advertise as in
the seventh thousand. This was a popular, somewhat
naïve production, which, after a few snippets of general
information, devoted most of its twenty pages to an
almanack of encouragement to the converted. The reminder that February 24th is the awesome anniversary of
the birth of the Duke of Cambridge, in 1774, is followed
by '*25.* 60,000 drunkards die annually,' an ambiguous
announcement that leaves us uncertain as to whether, in
the face of so awful an holocaust, this day is particularly
fatal to those who drink or whether it should be celebrated
as All Soaks Day. It is equally difficult to decide why July
17th and 18th should be bracketed together with the dire
monition 'Awake, drunkards, and howl for the miseries
coming upon you.' The last page proclaims that 'Advertisers who have anything to say to the sober portion of the
community, will find this a valuable medium of communication.' It cannot, however, have been of great
value to its editor and proprietor for the ten shillings
asked for a whole-page advertisement was later reduced to
eight.

Cook, the publisher, was also concerned at this time
with temperance hymn-books. Possibly the earliest of
these was *Hymns for Temperance Meetings, more specially
designed for Meetings in the Open Air.* These twenty-one

* *Temperance History*, Dawson Burns, D.D., i. 203.

effusions mostly dwell, with extreme satisfaction, on the doom of

> 'Drunkards, juvenile or hoary,
> Male or female, black or white'

in their grim procession:

> 'Six hundred thousand drunkards march
> To wretchedness and hell;
> While loud laments, and tears, and groans,
> In dismal chorus swell.'

This unctuous pennyworth also promises, as 'preparing for publication' *The National Temperance and Rechabite Hymn Book*, the announcement of which throws a light on current editorial practice. Thomas Cook did not unduly concern himself with author's rights. 'For the accommodation of those who use Beardsall's Selection, the Hymns which are copied from that book, will be so arranged as to be easily referred to.... Original Hymns will be thankfully received by the Publisher, T. Cook, Leicester: and, if approved, copies of the book will be given in exchange for them.' This method, which suggests that Thomas Cook might have been a successful anthologist in this century, even also served in the compilation of *The National Temperance Hymn Book and Rechabite Songster* of 1843. This, 'the largest Temperance Hymn Book ever published,' contained 'the cream of all the selections extant (which are public property) besides upwards of two hundred Original Hymns' and could be had, at from eightpence to eighteenpence, in various bindings.

To his list Cook also added pamphlets of particular interest to his fellow-Baptists, such as a reprint of *The Itinerant*, by Samuel Deacon, the famous Barton minister, whose homely verses, first published in 1815, must have recalled to Cook his own experiences as a village evangelist; and a commemorative publication on *The Barton Centenary* in 1845, compiled by himself. But much of the

Baptist work was in the hands of his friend, J. F. Winks, who had settled in Leicester, in 1839, two years before Cook arrived there.

A few such general publications as might be expected from a provincial printing office came from the Midland Temperance Press. As, for example, *The Celestial Messenger and Midland Counties Weather Guide*, compiled by *Mercurius and Herschell*, a formidable collaboration worth any rustic sixpence; and *The Leicester Almanac and Guide to Leicester*, a shilling publication. But the most historically interesting of Cook's local publications would seem to have been his Leicester street-directory. According to a contributor of *The Illustrated Leicester Chronicle*, 'he invented a new style in street-directories which has been the model of all directories ever since.'

The imprint of the Midland Temperance Press had appeared for barely three years on the publications by which Cook sought to serve the interests of the spreading causes he adopted, before he began to develop that other interest which, in the end, was to transform the local pundit into the household word.

CHAPTER EIGHT

We Travel On

THE 'amateur performances,' as the great excursionist afterwards described those early excursions, which served temperance enthusiasts and Sunday school children, began in time to point towards an altogether new ambition, towards Good Business as an end in itself— a laudable aim for the righteous as for the ungodly nineteenth-century man. There was evidently a wider public eager to take advantage of excursions. Though he had not been the only one to organize them, his name was becoming more widely, and gratifyingly, associated with this new, cheap facility which was bringing freedom of movement to so many to whom it had hitherto been denied. Had not even the London papers remarked 'that the Midlands Company were carrying passengers, by Cook's excursions, one hundred miles for a shilling?' By 1844, these arrangements alone, which he made gratuitously, took up most of his summer time. He himself had proclaimed, with all the emphasis that capitals could give, 'We must have RAILWAYS FOR THE MILLION.'

Yet, if the Million were to be served by the organization of pleasure trips, how could he afford, however altruistic his prime motive, to be disinterested?

When, therefore, he came to his decision to establish a new business as 'excursion-agent,' it was on the basis of an arrangement with the directors of the Midland Railway whereby they agreed 'to place trains at his disposal while he provided the passengers.' W. Fraser Rae (1891), the official jubilee biographer, does not mention the basis of Cook's remuneration. It is generally and most probably stated that this was a percentage on fares. But an article in *Chambers's Journal*, November 29th, 1852, states: 'There ... are middlemen, who have a train on speculation, and make the best they can out of it. . . . Mr. Cook, of Leicester, is perhaps the leader among these excursion projectors.'

Cook's entry into the business may have involved an act of faith in the potentialities and future development of steam transport—that was contagious enough in those days of the railway mania—as much as a mere acceptance of their present achievement. Already, by 1845, the date of Thomas Cook's first pleasure-trip, the railways had exerted a compelling influence on the English way of life. He was not, of course, directly concerned with their economic effects on industry and commerce or with their benefits to agriculture. His plans, however, depended somewhat on the increased general prosperity consequent on these, so that all but the very poor could afford to take advantage of the mobility suddenly conferred on them.

He saw the railways as a social force. His excursions and tours were projected on a near-Benthamite principle of the greatest benefit for the greatest number at the lowest cost. The last factor depended on inducing those railway directors who had not already discovered it for themselves that it was more profitable to carry the maximum of passengers at reduced rates than a few at normal fares.

In 1860, out of his experience, he gave an account of the *Physical, Moral, and Social Aspects of Excursions and Tours*, in which he writes: 'In an interesting correspondence that I once had with Eliza Cook* . . . that talented and high-

* Alas, talent and high spirits are not enough. This amiable poetaster, 1818-89, who was unrelated to the excursionist, is now remembered only by the amateurs of bad verse and that chiefly in respect of *The Old Arm Chair*, a fly preserved in the imitation amber of Henry Russell's setting.

spirited lady wrote her strong approval of Excursions, inasmuch as their tendency is to "unite man to man, and man to God." ' . . . This is a view of the case that ranks among the most interesting results of my own experience. It is delightful to see, as we travel on, the breaking down of partition walls of prejudice, the subduing of evil passions and unhappy tempers, the expansion of the intellect, the grasping for information, the desire for books and the eagerness of their perusal, the benevolent sympathies excited by a more extended knowledge of the circumstances and sufferings of fellow creatures, the improvement in health and prospects, the endurance of fatigue, and, perseverance under difficulties . . .' He concludes like a moral auctioneer 'with numerous other indescribable influences of a happy and beneficial tendency.'

Perhaps Cook felt that another 'influence of a happy and beneficial tendency of assisted travel' were better omitted from so prim a catalogue. He does, however, suggest elsewhere: 'How often has it been that a young gentleman has taken a through ticket to some distant place, and ere he got half-way through his intended journey some fair charmer has unwittingly drawn him in another direction, or he has met with agreeable companions and longed to go with them.'*

Cook's manifestation in all this of one aspect of the Victorian temper was without doubt sincere. It is obviously of a piece with his evangelical fervour. Doubtless it was sincerely accepted, and encouraged, by many of his clients. Others, less earnestly, may have been taking a mere holiday.

Holidays were no new thing: by the eighteen-forties an annual holiday was becoming part of family life for those who could afford it. With the lower middle- and working-classes, nevertheless, the association of holidays with travel

* *Cook's Scottish Tourist*: A Handbook, etc., 1858, p. 8, where he describes how his tourists under such circumstances may change their routes, without incurring a loss on the tickets.

Five Days' Trip to the West of England

T. COOK, Excursion Agent, Leicester, has received authority from the Directors to announce a

CHARMING EXCURSION

TO

CHELTENHAM, GLOUCESTER,

BRISTOL,

EXETER & PLYMOUTH.

TUESDAY, JUNE 18, 1850,

SPECIAL TRAINS

Will run from NOTTINGHAM and LEICESTER and thence to BURTON, where they will be united and attached to a Train from Macclesfield, and proceed, *via* Birmingham, to Bristol.

TIME OF STARTING AND FARES THERE AND BACK.

PLACES and TIME of STARTING.	To Cheltenham or Gloucester.			To BRISTOL.		
	1st.	2nd.	3rd.	1st.	2nd.	3rd.
Nottingham, 8-40 a.m. ; Leicester, 8-30 ; Ashby, 9-20.	12s. 6d.	9s.	7s.	18s.	12s. 6d.	9s. 6d.
Derby, 9-30 ; Burton, 10 ; Tamworth, 10-30	11s. 6d.	8s. 6d.	6s. 6d.	17s.	12s.	9s.

A SPECIAL TRAIN WILL LEAVE BRISTOL FOR EXETER & PLYMOUTH,

On *WEDNESDAY MORNING, JUNE* 19th, at 7 a.m.

FARES from BRISTOL to EXETER & BACK :—First Class, 12s. Second Class, 8s. Third Class, 7s.
FROM EXETER to PLYMOUTH & BACK :—First Class, 7s. Second Class, 5s. 6d. (No Third.)

Passengers may return from Plymouth to Exeter, or Exeter to Bristol, by the ordinary Trains (Express and Mails excepted) on payment of an extra Shilling to each company, at any time previous to the hour fixed for the return of the Special Train, which will leave Plymouth at 3-30 p.m., and Exeter at 6 on Friday, June 21.

The Train will return from Bristol on Saturday June 22, at 9 a.m. : from Gloucester at 10-30 : and from Cheltenham at 10-45. Passengers may return on Friday, June 21, on payment of 1s. extra, by the Trains leaving Bristol at 11 a.m. Gloucester at 12-35, p.m. Cheltenham at 12-55, and Birmingham at 3-30.

TICKETS are issued at the Stations and any additional particulars may be had on application by letter, with stamp for reply, to the Manager of the Trip,—T. COOK, 28, Granby-street, Leicester.

T. COOK will be in attendance at GIRAUD'S Victoria Temperance Hotel, Corner of Bath-street, Bristol, on Tuesday Evening, after the arrival of the Special Train, for the purpose of issuing Tickets for Exeter and Plymouth.

N.B.—By the arrangements of this Trip, Tourists will be introduced to districts full of natural, artistical, commercial and historical interest and importance. The bare mention of the names of the deeply interesting Cities of CHELTENHAM, GLOUCESTER, BRISTOL, BATH, EXETER, &c., call up a thousand pleasing associations which cannot be set forth in a handbill. Visitors to Cheltenham will have the privilege of attending the Great HORTICULTURAL EXHIBITION, which takes place on the 20th Instant. From Bristol, River and Sea Trips may be made to CHEPSTOW, TENBY, and other places of note on the Western Coast. Excursions may also be made to various places in SOUTH WALES, such as MONMOUTH, TINTERN ABBEY, &c. &c. The Plymouth tourist will be conveyed over the most astonishing Railway in the world, running along the Coast, over Crags, Promontories, &c. extending into the sea. The Docks, Arsenal, Fortifications, &c. of PLYMOUTH and DEVONPORT, will be viewed with intense interest; and should the tourist desire to reach the "Land's End" in Cornwall, he may accomplish that object, and return in time to avail himself of an arrangement of the Manager of the Trip, in the month of July, for an Excursion to "John o' Groat's House," at the extreme northern point of Scotland ! Such are the glorious facilities afforded by Railways and Steamboats. Let the people appreciate and rejoice in them !

T. COOK, PRINTER, 28, GRANBY-STREET, LEICESTER.

still had an element of novelty. Holiday travel was greatly accelerated by the new railways, but had begun before their introduction, with the plying of pleasure-steamers from the larger coastal places and on navigable rivers. These were first used on the Clyde. They were introduced on the Thames in 1815 when trips to Gravesend were inaugurated, being soon followed by others, celebrated by Charles Lamb and Charles Dickens, to Margate and Ramsgate. The total of 105,625 passengers to these last two places in the record year of 1835-36, indicates the popularity of these jaunts. Thomas Cook availed himself of both steamers and trains in the first pleasure-trips he arranged.

In the summer of 1845, after negotiations with the four railway companies involved, he announced a pleasure-trip by special train from Leicester, Nottingham and Derby to Liverpool and back. The fare was fourteen shillings, first-class, and ten shillings, second-class. There was no third-class accommodation. A supplementary—that smooth purposeful word which has triumphantly run the gamut from the printer's desk in Leicester to the polished counters of the Berkeley Street headquarters to-day—was made whereby excursionists could proceed by the steamer *Eclipse* to Carnarvon, by way of Bangor and the Menai Straits, and another for those who wished to scale Snowdon on 'Shanks' naggie.' The advertisement of the trip, says Cook, caused a sensation. All tickets were sold a week before the event and many changed hands at a premium.

Cook made his preparations with a thoroughness that was to establish a precedent. Fraser Rae tells us that he 'did not content himself with providing tickets at low prices for pleasure-seekers, and making such arrangements as should ensure that they would be carried by rail or steamer to their destination in comfort and safety. Before any trip was advertised, he visited the towns where stoppages were to be made, and personally ascertained whether there were any sights, and also what hotels accommodated travellers of moderate means.' This latter was, in those early days of railroad travel, a most necessary precaution. Previously, the coaching inns had been able to put up a few road passengers without difficulty. Several hundred excursionists pouring from a train at the same time posed a new problem which it was Cook's job to solve. Nor did his preliminary work stop here. For this first trip, as later, he compiled and printed a small guide, 'containing notices of the places of interest on the way, and the sights which were to be visited.' More than sixty years ago, Fraser Rae described this *Handbook of the Trip to Liverpool* as a curiosity in the literature of travel. It is, he says, 'noteworthy for the minuteness of the information which its compiler supplied; everything is laudably precise and clear, and the opening sentences afford examples of this: "The Train will leave Leicester at Five o'clock in the morning of Monday, August the 4th, reaching Syston at Ten minutes past Five; Sileby, Twenty minutes past Five; Loughborough, Half-past Five; Kegworth, a Quarter before Six; arriving at Derby at Ten Minutes past Six. A train will leave Nottingham at Half-past Five, uniting with the Leicester train at Derby. Parties will have to be 'wide-awake' at an early hour, or they will be disappointed. Promptitude on the part of the Railway Company calls for the same from passengers." ' The three hundred and fifty excursionists formed the largest pleasure party ever to land at Carnarvon, where only one Welshman with sufficient English could be found to act as guide.

The demand for tickets for this trip had been so much beyond the capacity of the rolling stock available that Cook decided to run a second, identical with the first, a fortnight later. He was told that these two excursions were the first to be dealt with by the Railway Clearing House, which by common agreement had been established by the railways in 1842 to deal with the accounts of through transactions. It is not this incidental fact, however, that gives the excursion of August 4th, 1845, its significance. I diffidently suggest that this date rather than the much-vaunted excursion of July, 1841, marks the effective beginnings of the firm of Thos. Cook & Son.

The pioneering claim advanced for Thomas Cook in respect of his first Leicester-Loughborough excursion pales into tentativeness. His 'personal conducting' on that occasion was little more than a gentle shepherding. But in his handling of the arrangements for the first pleasure-trip to Liverpool, there is nothing tentative. He had learned much from his 'amateur performances,' but even apart from the question of financial interest, their time was over. He now showed so firm a grasp of the essentials of his job that these first arrangements established the general pattern of all those since made by the firm, which only differs from the earlier ones in their scale and scope. Only mischance could temporarily divert his plans though not upset his quiet assurance.

On the second Liverpool trip, he tells us, 'We reached the Menai Bridge in the dusk of the evening, and the Captain refused to attempt the navigation of the Straits till daylight. The chief of the party refused to leave the boat for the night, and a strange scene of excitement ensued. At about 11 a.m. next day we landed at Carnarvon, and had to return in about an hour, to reach Liverpool in time for the return special train. But despite all these drawbacks to comfort, the trip was heartily enjoyed by most of the Tourists.'

If Cook was to be successful in this new wonderful profession, he must enlarge his territory. He could not afford to wait on the extension of the railways but must foster the demand for travel and satisfy it as best he might with existing facilities, leaving the railways to follow. While in North Wales, he caught a gleam of his next adventure and entered a resolve in his diary: 'From the heights of Snowdon my thoughts took flight to Ben Lomond, and I determined to try to get to Scotland.' That is, he was going 'to try to get' as many as possible of those

who could afford his modest charges to share in the
benefits of 'associated travel' in a country whose visitors
had hitherto been mainly of the opulent and leisured
classes.

Scotland's vogue among English tourists had vastly
increased since the numbers of those in search of the
picturesque had been swollen by the admirers of Burns
and, more particularly, of Scott. From 1810, when *The
Lady of the Lake* was first published, as each Waverley
novel appeared, more and more tourists flooded over the
border to visit the settings of the poems and novels.

It was probably their shared enthusiasm for Scott that
first drew Queen Victoria and Prince Albert to Scotland
where, from 1842, they made holiday and thus helped to
develop a loyal tourist trend.

Early in 1846, Thomas Cook made two exploratory
visits to Scotland. His most obvious difficulty was that
Newcastle was then the northern limit of the railway. Nor
was there a through line from Leicester to Newcastle. The
indomitable Cook might have overcome these obstacles—
'the Napoleon of excursions' was not to be defeated in a
skirmish—but he could not break down the resistance
shown to his scheme by the proprietors of the steamship
service between the Tyne and Leith, in spite of his offer of
a guarantee. Willy-nilly he had to devise a western route.
He therefore arranged for railway transport from Leicester
to Fleetwood, thence to Ardrossan by steamer, resuming
the railway from Ardrossan to Glasgow and so on to
Edinburgh. His next job was to advertise his excursion for
Midsummer, 1846, and to get ready a *Handbook of a Trip to
Scotland* with 'such information, as he conceives, will be
found most useful for those who avail themselves of a
privilege which no previous generation ever had offered to
them—an opportunity of riding from Leicester to Glasgow
and back, a distance of about 800 miles, for a guinea!'

Three hundred and fifty accepted this remarkable offer.
They got to Fleetwood in excellent order and boarded the

steamer for a night-crossing of the Irish Sea. It was a dirty night and soon, when the unhappy excursionists sought the shelter of their cabins, discovery was made that Cook had booked too many first-class passengers for the available accommodation. He had at first conditionally engaged a special boat of ample capacity which was to be chartered by a given day if he could guarantee a sufficient number of passengers. Tickets had gone somewhat slowly at first and he had decided to rely on the ordinary accommodation. Cook had an even more uncomfortable night than the malcontents.

Their ill-humour, however, began to disperse as the special train from Ardrossan sped towards Glasgow. It vanished entirely in the excitement of their welcome. Guns were fired in their honour as the train drew up to the platform. They were met with a band of music and thus escorted to the City Hall. There a soirée was held and they were entertained to 'noble speeches' including one, an hour long, on 'The Natural, Moral and Political Effects of Temperance.' This arduous pursuit of pleasure begins to seem uncommonly like a temperance gala writ large. It should be remarked, however, that Cook, if never loth to improve a moral occasion, did not attempt, either on this occasion or afterwards, to rigidly impose his own principles on others. He thus differed from one of his later competitors, John Frame, also an ardent teetotaller, whose first tour, in 1881, was in connection with a temperance demonstration, and who generally insisted on strict temperance rules for his clients.

Even Glasgow eloquence ends at last. Cook, on the morrow, led his excursionists forward to Edinburgh to another tumultuous reception. William Chambers, the famous publisher, presided at another soirée, in the Waterloo Rooms, and gave an address which Cook, who also made a speech, diplomatically suggested should be published. Which it was, a few weeks later, under the title of *The Strangers' Visit to Edinburgh*. The strangers were

entertained to a concert of accordion and piano playing
and then at last let go about their business as excursionists.
They went to Stirling by the Forth steamers. They sailed
on Loch Lomond—Cook must have remembered his
Snowdon resolution. They went by train to Burns'
Ayrshire. Then, satisfied with his modest success, medi-
tating larger and more extended excursions for the seasons
to come, Cook went home to Leicester.

CHAPTER NINE

The Field Marshal

ENTERPRISE—and eloquence—were opening new vistas for Thomas Cook. The revelation neither obscured nor obliterated his continuing, if variable, vision. Whatever might be the prospects of commercial development, he was never loath to succour or indeed to save his fellow men. In this respect, I do not see him as a giant, but rather as a worthy, raised by his energy head and shoulders above his fellows within a potent but modest loyalized pattern. *A Tract for the Winter of* 1845-6, was a first of a series of *Monthly Tracts for the Times*. Encouraged by Cook, the cries of 'Cheap Bread for the Million!' and 'An honest four-pound loaf for every purchaser!' began to ring out in Leicester streets.

Let his own account light this episode: '. . . in connection with the repeal of the Corn Laws, I took a very active part in promoting interest and excitement among the people. I published a little paper called *The Cheap Bread Herald* in which my main object was to accelerate the downfall of Protection, and during those months it was my practice on every Monday and Friday evening to make announcements from my window in Granby Street of the state of the markets and other matters connected with Corn Law Appeal. On such evenings, there generally collected together about a thousand people to listen to my statements from the public window of my house, and during most of the time I had the satisfaction of issuing and exposing placards headed 'Down Again,' as prices continued to fall. A committee was formed to work with me and very strenuous efforts were made to compel the bakers and breadsellers to sell by weight, and much excitement was created in the town. One Monday morning we sent out a number of men to purchase a loaf from every baker and breadseller in Leicester; the loaves were ticketed with the name of the shop where each was bought and the price paid, and in the evening, in response to an invitation by placard, at least two thousand people assembled in the Amphitheatre in Humberstone Gate to witness a public Assize of Bread. The loaves bought were brought on to the platform, and by permission of the Town Clerk, the borough scales were used to weigh the bread loaf by loaf. The weight was announced, being in some instances but little over 3 lbs. for the 4-lb. loaf. The names of the dealers and their prices were all published, and great excitement was caused in the trade, but the magistrates were with us and enforced numerous fines—not only of the omission to weigh the loaves, but also for adulteration. In connection with the Protection agitation, an incident occurred which may be worth recording. I received a summons calling upon me to go to the Court of Exchequer to answer certain charges which would be there brought against me in connection with the publication of the little paper I have referred to. I wrote a statement of my motives and went up to London and presented the statement to the solicitor of Inland Revenue at Somerset House, who told me that the Board of Commissioners was then sitting. He took in my letter, and came out, stating that the Board, seeing that the objects I had in view were of a benevolent character, agreed to withdraw the summons on payment by me of a sovereign, which would not cover the expenses incurred. He told me I was at perfect liberty to say what I liked in my paper about Whigs or Tories. I might denounce them all if I liked, but if I touched the revenue they would touch me. All that I had done was to insert in my paper a short paragraph referring to the French Revolution, and that being deemed general news, I was threatened with prosecution under the Stamp Act.'

The odious Stamp Act not having been repealed until 1861, *The Cheap Bread Herald* must have been one of the unstamped publications prevented from printing any item of news under pain of heavy penalties. The incident serves to show Cook not only as a man of purpose but also as a man of the world in the making. No doubt his appearance at Somerset House was something of an adventure even to one accustomed to proclaim from a window in Granby Street, Leicester. He was to record for *The Times* that 'this going round the world is a very easy and almost imperceptible business,' and the world was to marvel at his two hundred and twenty-two days' pioneer globe-girdling excursion. But in the late 'forties, his horizons were still contained by the British Isles.

Early in 1847, he conducted a second excursion to Scotland by the same route as in the previous year. That and subsequent excursions may have failed to evoke the heady Scots enthusiasm that had greeted his first party, but his arrangements became steadily more comfortable as his experience grew. Later, in the autumn of 1847, he availed himself of the newly-opened Newcastle-Berwick line, to run a special train from Manchester and other places to Edinburgh direct. In Scotland itself he extended his scope. 'I followed the Queen and Prince Albert over the route which they made royal, by the Clyde, the Kyles of Bute, the Crinan Canal, and the Atlantic Coast to Oban; from thence to Staffa and Iona, circumnavigating the island of Mull and afterwards visiting Glendor, Fort William and the Caledonian Canal to Inverness. The great Highland coach road between Inverness, Dunkeld and Perth became a favourite route long ere the first sod of a railway was turned.' Thus royalty disclosed an affinity for

Scotland and gave to tourism its first tartan period which a later century—of royalty and tourists—has so eagerly emulated.

Cook now initiated his 'first great combinations of special tickets for circular tours,' a facility at first restricted to his large excursion parties, but later extended. From 1848 until 1863, with the exception of 1851, when he was otherwise too busy, he spent two months of each summer conducting parties to and through Scotland. His four annual great excursions, with a total of some five thousand visitors a season, alternated between the east and west routes 'so as to hold the balance as evenly as possible between the Companies interested in Scotch Traffic.' For the purpose of his excursions, Cook welded the railway, steamer and coaching facilities of the country into one extended tourist arrangement, providing tickets for the whole or any part of the more than two thousand miles covered.

Something of the atmosphere of 'associated travel' under Cook's ægis, and a sidelight on the rigours of early railway-travelling can be gathered from a diary, I believe unpublished, extracts from which were made for the firm's museum. Edward Chadfield of Derby made an excursion to Scotland in 1849. With his brother and a friend, he left Derby in the early morning of July 24th, and reached Edinburgh 'in the dark and rain' late that night after nothing more untoward than delays caused by broken coupling-chains.

'Wednesday, July 25th, 1849. We now commenced our peregrinations in Edinburgh by going to meet Mr. Cook and the excursionists. We sauntered about here very comfortably in a drizzling rain for about half an hour before Mr. Cook arrived, and after a little speechifying we divided into parties of fifty, appointing a captain to each party. We all paid a shilling each to our Captain, who hired a guide, and then we went sightseeing.

'After returning to Edinburgh, we went to a meeting at

the Calton Convening Rooms where the excursionists were to fraternize with the "cannie Scotch." However, we found no sawnies to fraternize with, so after a good deal of bad speaking, and tolerable singing, and heaps of fun and laughing, we dispersed.'

The next day the party went by special train to Glasgow, leaving Edinburgh at 7 a.m. On the way they visited Linlithgow ('where we sang "God Save the Queen" from the top of the ruined towers') and Stirling: 'On arriving at Stirling Junction our train ran up twelve miles to Stirling, and we immediately started for the Castle. We soon mounted the hill, and stormed the castle, the soldiers opening their eyes too wide at our numbers to think of opposing us. We sprung on the walls, and oh what a glorious country lay opened out at our feet . . .'

That afternoon the excursionists made the journey from Glasgow to Ayr, to see Burns' birthplace: 'As we were going on full speed, thirty-six or thirty-seven miles an hour, we all felt a great check to the train and the next moment we were all chucked half-way to the top of the carriage. As soon as we found our legs we put our heads out of the window and discovered the train just stopping, and a brownish mass lying on the railway some hundred yards behind us. We jumped out on the line, and we then saw that two of the carriages were off the rails and had been ploughing along famously. We ran back and found the brownish heap was the remains of a horse, completely smashed and cut up by the train. But, worse than that, we saw one of the guards lying at the bottom of the embankment, to all appearance dead. On enquiry we found that the horse had strayed on the line just in front of the engine and the shock of the carriage the guards were sitting on,*

---

* The guards on early railway trains usually sat on the outside of the carriage. The head guard on the last carriage faced forwards and the underguard on the first carriage looked backwards. They could thus be certain that the complete train was following, a desirable precaution when coupling-chains frequently snapped and carriages had a tendency to get left behind.

passing over the horse, had thrown one right from the top of the carriage to the bottom of the embankment. The poor fellow's head was dreadfully gashed, and he was insensible for some time, and the first thing he did before enquiring anything about himself was to ask if the passengers were safe; fine fellow, in the midst of his own pain and weakness, to think of the passengers. We managed to lift the carriages on the rails again, and were soon on our way . . .'

Thomas Cook's boasted immunity from accident to his excursionists was evidently a near thing at times. His present batch returned to Glasgow where 'We went to Mr. Cook for tickets for Loch Lomond and then to our beds at Whyte's Temperance Hotel, Irongate, Glasgow.'

The following day was given to an excursion down the Clyde and the ascent of Ben Lomond and the next after to a visit to the Trossachs. Then:

Sunday, July 29th. 'After lunch at the Inn, we walked to Callander, ten miles. . . . At Callander we had an amusing scene with the rival coachmen. It appeared that there were two opposition coaches . . . and seeing our party of twelve, both parties were anxious to secure us. The result was that our own coach took us for one shilling per head, the regular fare being three shillings.'

On the morrow Chadwick and his friends were 'off by the coach to Stirling,' whence they sailed down the Forth to Cranton Pier, and there boarded a train for Edinburgh. Their last day in Scotland was spent in visiting Portobello and Leith, whence they returned to their Edinburgh hotel to find that 'some Scotchmen had joined our party, for the purpose of bidding good-bye, and both English and Scotch were all singing like so many larks, full merry enough too. All sorts of invitations were given to All Scotland and All England to call upon them at their respective houses. However, we were soon off to bed for the last time in Scotland.'

Then, like so many larks again, they were up betimes,

so that they caught the six o'clock train to England. The tedium of the long journey was enlivened by a carriage catching alight at Berwick and the aversion of a collision with a coal train at Newcastle by a matter of yards. A forty-five minutes' wait at York enabled them to ferry across the Ouse, 'do' the city and the Minster, and get something to eat. They arrived 'safe at Derby soon after eleven o'clock having travelled a thousand miles in two hundred and seven hours for an expense of five pounds ten shillings.'

A fuller, if more objective account of Cook's Scottish arrangements, which varied little year by year, appeared in *Chambers's Edinburgh Journal* in 1853, and helps to fill in details. 'The Midland excursions to the north under Mr. Cook's management are really very curious, and deserving of attention; for an attempt is made to gather up tourists from a number of tributary streams, then carry them in a body along a trunk-line of railway, and then distribute them over the north, to catch pleasure wherever it is to be found. Then, the pleasure being over, the wanderers are picked up from far and wide, they are brought back along the trunk-line of railway, and they are distributed over the whole of the south, almost to their own doors . . .

'First, then, it may be well to remember that the Midland Railway has a main trunk-line from Derby northwards to Leeds and York; that at the north end it joins other lines which extend towards and into Scotland; and that, at the south end, it is connected with many branching lines, some belonging to the same and some to other companies. These southern branches have stations at numerous important towns, the dwellers in which may wish—some to visit the midland counties, and some to have a peep at the regions beyond the Tweed. Field-Marshal Cook, then—for we can scarcely refuse military honour to one who manœuvres large bodies of men in such a way—undertakes to convey the midlanders

to Scotland, and the southerners to the Midlands and to
Scotland; and he has to time his movements with no
little forethought, to ensure that none shall be kept
waiting for the others. On a particular day, the Londoners
are taken down to numerous stations on the Midland line;
those for the far north making a temporary sojourn at
Derby;* the Essex, Norfolk, and Suffolk folks reach
Leicester by way of Peterborough and Syston Railway;
the Lincoln and Newark inhabitants advance as far as
Nottingham; the Rugby, and Leamington, and Coventry
people reach Leicester by the Midland; while the
Worcester, Cheltenham, Gloucester, and Bristol pleasure-
seekers advance as far north as Birmingham. Very early
next morning, three trains start from Birmingham,
Leicester, and Nottingham, respectively, taking all these
loads of tourists, and coming to a grand meeting-point at
Derby. At seven o'clock, off they go, forming one train
(very like *monstre*) of persons from perhaps twenty southern
counties. The train picks up and sets down at Chesterfield,
Sheffield, Normanton, York, Newcastle, Berwick, and
other stations, and finally arrives at the Scotch metropolis
the same evening.

'Here they are, then: the Britons have invaded Scotland;
and now, what will they do? We have the field-marshal's
printed programme before us, and a very curious
programme it is. On the first night, the Britons sleep in
Edinburgh, each one catering for himself. On the following
morning, they all meet at the Calton Hill "to arrange
the party in divisions, and form plans for the day.' . . .
Supposing the journey from England to have been made
on Wednesday, the morning of Thursday is devoted to
the Calton council, followed by visits to the Castle, Holy-
rood, and other notabilities in and around Edinburgh;

* Some of the sojourners at Derby were doubtless accommodated at
Smithard's Temperance Hotel, Corn Market, an enterprise which later,
less grandiloquently, became Simeon Smithard's Private Temperance
Boarding House, Gerrard Street. Cook himself could offer accommodation
at Leicester.

and at one o'clock they start off by the North British Railway to Melrose, have a peep at the Abbey, then go by the next train to St. Boswell's, then walk to Dryburgh and back to Edinburgh the same evening. Friday next arrives and with it a busy day's work, for which long daylight and fine weather are needed. A special train starts betimes from Edinburgh to Glasgow, where an hour is then left to enable the Britons to get snugly on board a steamer at the Broomislaw; they start down the Clyde to Dowling, then take the little railway to Balloch, then steam up Loch Lomond to Tarbet, next walk over to Arrochar, at the head of Loch Long, and then steam down Loch Long to the Clyde and Glasgow; 100 miles' sailing, railing, and walking through the most enchanting scenery of Scotland, all for 4s.—so says the programme. Saturday is devoted to the Oban trip, down the Firth, through the Kyles of Bute, and over Loch Fyne, to Ardrishaig; thence by the Crinan Canal, and past the whirlpool of Corrievreck to Oban. "This," says the programme, "is a lovely spot for repose, amid most beautiful scenery, and a charming place for weary tourists. It will be our home for two or three days, and lodgings are wonderfully cheap."

'On Sunday, the Britons remain quiet at Oban. On Monday, they make the trip to the Isle of Skye; and each tourist is requested to read, before he starts, the *Lord of the Isles*, to prepare him for what he is about to see. Tuesday is appropriated to the Staffa trip: "We hope that the day may be favourable for rowing into the cave; but if this is impracticable, we shall still land at Staffa, and again at Iona, there to ruminate amidst the ruins of that ancient seat of learning, and tombs of kings, warriors, chieftains, and ecclesiastics. Tourists! go with us to Staffa and Iona, the strongest sensibilities of your natures shall be awakened!" On Wednesday, the field-marshal returns to Glasgow, and thence to England; but leaves his brother Britons to make out a full fortnight as they best choose.'

I have lingered thus over the details of Cook's Scottish

tours because they were the staple of his business as 'excursion-agent' and 'tourist-manager' in the earlier days, and because they were not only the first, but were generally representative of all the other 'arrangements' that he then made. One other detail should be noticed. It concerns what Cook, writing after twenty years' experience, describes as 'the oft-reiterated question: Is it safe and proper for ladies to join in Highland tours?' To which he replies that 'of the thousands of tourists who have travelled with us, the majority have been ladies. In family parties, the preponderance is generally on the feminine side; but there are also great numbers of ladies who start alone, and always meet with agreeable company and get through without any particular inconvenience or discomfort.

'As to their energy, bravery, and endurance of toil, as a rule they are fully equal to those of the opposite sex, whilst many of them frequently put to shame the "masculine" effeminates.

'. . . The trappings of prevailing fashion may sometimes perplex them in climbing over precipices, and amongst rude blocks of granite and basalt; but there is a large class, who, defiant of fashion or customs . . . push their way through all difficulties, and acquire the perfection of tourist character.'

No greater compliment, I feel, was ever intended by Thomas Cook in his character of tourist and excursionist. It was perhaps tinged with tribute to his wife, for Mrs. Cook frequently accompanied her husband on these early tours (was she regarded as chaperone to the venturesome lone ladies of the parties?), putting aside for a few days the cares of hotel management in Leicester and delegating the charge of her second child, a daughter, Annie Elizabeth, who had been born in 1845.

CHAPTER TEN

The Practical Idealist

SINCE the Second World War, the opening up of ancestral homes has proved to be a popular addition to the tourist attractions of Great Britain. Declining wealth and the prodigious cost of upkeep, as all the world knows, have created this pleasing new branch of the tourist industry which, in the satisfaction it gives all round, is surely preferable to the wholesale breaking-up which followed the First World War.

A hundred years ago, the ancestral homes were in their heyday, many of them still looking forward to increased wealth and grandeur which several decades of British industrial expansion were to bestow upon them. Nevertheless, the idea that the masses might from time to time have a glimpse of the opulent life of their betters had some currency in those times. Did not Tennyson write:

'Why should not these great Sirs
Give up their parks some dozen times a year
To let the people breathe?'

I do not suggest that our ever-prolific prose-writing Thomas Cook dipped into the new poetry of his eminent contemporary to obtain inspiration for new excursion ideas. Yet, after extending his activities to the Lake District, North Wales, the Isle of Man and Ireland in the late eighteen-forties, he began to approach, not always with success, some of the great landowners in the Midlands with a view to their throwing open their parks to 'let the people breathe.' The people he had in mind were industrial workers in Leicester and thereabouts. In 1848, the Duke of Rutland opened Belvoir Castle to Cook's excursionists who, in the absence of a railway, went there by horse-drawn coach. Another noble arrangement—and it was to have significant repercussions for Cook—was that by which the Duke of Devonshire welcomed trainloads of workers who descended upon Chatsworth. At that time, Joseph Paxton, who had begun his working life, like Thomas Cook, as a garden-boy, had already, by means of his inventive genius, worked himself up to the position of agent to the Duke. No doubt it was he with whom the arrangements were made, thus providing an introduction which, as we shall learn later in this chapter, was to be of momentous value during the wonderful year of the Great Exhibition.

Cook got great pleasure from this phase of his activities. He delighted to tell how a 'poor working man' had approached him on York platform and ended words of thanks with "I wish I could tell the world how I feel of what we working people owe to you." He proudly recounted, too, how once, with a party of twelve hundred at Chatsworth: 'I stood at the gates and saw almost every one of them enter, and I remarked their conduct in returning home. There was no rudeness, no damage done to house or gardens, nor a drunken passenger to be seen as the party returned home'—a happy state of affairs he contrasted with that on working-class excursions in Scotland where 'day-trips are often occasions of drunken revelry.'

It must not be assumed, however, that the pattern of these years was one of smooth and effortless progress. He had made his conquests in highly competitive and expanding fields of transportation. His ideas were prolific, but they were not copyright. No doubt his outlook was provincial—as indeed he preferred it to remain, even in after years when he had girdled the globe. There were also material grounds for his present limitations. If he had not been able to include the whole of England and had done little for London and the South in making his arrangements, it was because he was only allowed to run two or three excursions a year over the London lines. Within his own territory, he was a name to be reckoned with, and his fame had spread to the Capital itself. By imagination and organizing ability, he had done much towards founding a new industry. In it, however, his prime place was by no means assured. He had not gained a monopoly by his excursions. Competition grew. The railway companies themselves were making excursion traffic, under the direction of excursion managers, a feature of their regular programme, thus limiting the professional scope of outside agents. Cook's arrangements with the companies were, moreover, on a short-term basis. As he looked about him and compared his activities with those of other industries in the Midlands, he may well have been daunted from time to time by the feeling that his progress was a hand-to-mouth affair depending essentially upon his own tireless energies and powers of extemporization. Each season his plans for the Scottish tours had to be approved by the committees that controlled traffic in Scotland, and there could be no firm certainty of their continuance. Probably most of his other work was on a similar seasonal basis.

Cook accepted the challenge. He believed he had sufficient advantages to meet ordinary competition. He had had a much wider experience of excursions and tours than any other man in the country. His successful conduct of these had won him the confidence of an increasing number, many of them first induced to travel by his blandishments, most of them finding travel with him easier, more comfortable, more economical, and more socially agreeable than by themselves. These, of course, were likely to return to him year after year. He would, of course, continue his excursions and trips in the British Isles.

Might it not be as well to look abroad, also? With mobility for the masses gained in the Midlands, should the adventure of travel overseas remain the perquisite of the few? The decision was not entirely a matter of business. Cook had converted others to the delights and benefits of travel. His greatest convert was Thomas Cook. 'Though circumscribed in plans of local operation,' he wrote, 'I had become so thoroughly imbued with the Tourist spirit, that I began to contemplate Foreign Trips, including the Continent of Europe, the United States, and the Eastern Lands of the Bible.' It is likely that his general plans for extended travel were influenced by James Silk Buckingham, whose advice he sought on the practicability of oriental travel. Buckingham was one of two national figures with whom Cook first made contact as a result of his work for temperance; the other was Father Mathew, the apostle of temperance. Buckingham (1786-1855), traveller, writer, M.P. for Sheffield, 1832-37, warm in all causes of reform and ardent in that of temperance, was chairman of the Select Committee to enquire into the Causes of Drunkenness, 1834. He lectured widely on temperance and delivered a two-hours' address at a Leicester demonstration on behalf of Father Mathew which Cook organized in 1844.

It may perhaps be noted here that the statement sometimes made, and included in *The Dictionary of National Biography*, that Thomas Cook was converted to total abstinence by Father Mathew is nonsense. The Rev. Theobald Mathew (1790-1856) did not himself sign the total abstinence pledge until April, 1838, sixteen months after Cook. His tremendously successful exertions in the cause of total abstinence were at first, with sufficient reason, confined to Ireland. He did not visit England until 1843, by which time Cook had been an active temperance worker for some years, and it was five years after that, in 1848, when Cook's first and only meeting with him took place, in the course of the excursionist's visit to Ireland, preliminary to his Irish tours.

Nevertheless, Cook was a great admirer of Father Mathew. He compiled and published, amongst other associated items, a pamphlet selection from his speeches. When Father Mathew had exhausted a considerable fortune in his work and was in difficulties, Cook took up the matter in his *National Temperance Magazine* and helped to initiate the public subscription which relieved him.

Meanwhile, during these years of consolidation, one can imagine something of the pattern of Cook's ever-increasing activities. His summer months were mostly given up to conducting the excursions and tours. Outside these there were new projects to be planned and publicized, exploratory visits to be made, negotiations to be conducted with railway companies, steamship owners, coach proprietors, and others. There were handbooks to be compiled and produced by his own printing office, in which the increasing excursionist requirements offset the decline in temperance and other publications.

There was no decline, however, in his temperance ardour. In 1849 he successfully revived an earlier scheme for building a Temperance Hall in Leicester, on a far more ambitious scale than he had formerly planned. He worked hard to raise funds for this darling project, but also found time actively to help in any other that promised improved wellbeing to his fellow-citizens of Leicester, particularly if it should stem from the temperance cause. It was probably the founding of Leicester Cottage Garden Allotment Society, with the support of the Rev. J. Babington (who had publicly signed the pledge after hearing an address by Thomas Cook), that led Cook to bring out under his own editorship *The Cottage Gardener*, which he described as 'a periodical of considerable size, which attracted great interest.'

THE METEOR. A MOTORCOACH TAKING A PARTY OF COOK'S TOURISTS TO VERSAILLES IN 1905

A COMET IS MET BY THE MAN FROM COOKS

Even Cook, with his zest for work and seeming ability
to forego sleep, could not have got through his many jobs
without some help. Many years on, after her death, he
was to pay grateful tribute to the way in which Mrs. Cook
had 'energetically assisted him to establish new businesses.'
We have seen that she frequently accompanied him on his
journeyings and that the running of the temperance hotel
was mostly her affair. But, as the travel scheme multiplied,
more work fell to the share of young John Mason, whom
we last left, a lad of ten or so, getting what schooling
he might between long hours in the printing office and
helpfully accompanying his father on the early excursions
for temperance societies and Sunday schools.

John Mason showed an eager, boyish interest in all
the details of these and an alacrity in mastering them.
Three years after he had been taken by his father on the
first memorable excursion of 1841, he was considered
experienced enough to share in the conduct of a children's
excursion. He later referred to 'my public career as a
Personal Conductor, which commenced in 1844, as a small
boy with a long wand assisting the guidance of 500 other
small children from Leicester to Syston by special train—
five miles; then two miles walk across the field, to the
Mount Sorrel Hills for an afternoon's picnic, and back
by the same route to Leicester.' After August, 1845, John
Mason accompanied his father on most of the extended
excursions, and these jaunts must have compensated him
to some extent for a lack-leisure boyhood. The pair set
off together on the 1845 tour of investigation which
preluded the Scottish tours, and when, in 1847, the York,
Newcastle and Berwick line was opened, making an east-
coast route available for the trips to Scotland, John Mason
was sent to Newcastle from Leicester a day ahead of the
party in order to conduct the first excursion train from
Newcastle to Scotland.

Although later it was expressly stipulated that a manager
must accompany the excursion trains in England and

D

Scotland, it does not appear to have been obligatory on Thomas Cook at first to produce an inspecting guard or conductor to travel with his trains. But 'his son voluntarily undertook the task, travelling with every train which ran over more than one company's line of railway. He had acquired such a knowledge of the various routes and junctions that he was regarded as an authority on the still-novel adventure of mass railroad travel. He was expert in the places where changes had to be made. At such junctions he was able to decide where the passengers' luggage was to be stowed, and he made a point of seeing it put in the proper van or on the roof of the carriage bound for the same place as the passengers in it. Thus his services were invaluable on the excursion trains running from the Eastern and Midland Counties to the Yorkshire watering-places, to Scotland and North Wales, to the West of England and the Land's End.'

These, of course, were only seasonal interruptions to a printer's progress. The great future of the elder Cook's enterprise was still undreamed of; and it was thought that John Mason should mainly depend on his printer's craft for a livelihood. It was considered desirable, too, that he should learn the business in an office other than his father's. Accordingly, the boy's fitful schooling was brought to an end before his fourteenth birthday, and he was sent to live with his grandmother, at Derby, in order that he might enter an office there on a six-months' trial before formally becoming an apprentice.

'At Derby,' Fraser Rae tells us, 'he was worked as hard or unmercifully as at Leicester. He left his grandmother's at six in the morning, walking a mile to the printing office, and carrying his breakfast with him. At midday he returned to dinner, and went back to work till eight in the evening. He was employed in setting books printed by the firm, and earned at least half the wages of a man. The firm was satisfied that he should continue to give his services on these terms, and when he pressed for a more satisfactory arrangement, it was agreed that he should become an apprentice. As such he was not to receive anything the first year. In the second year he was to be paid 1s. 6d. a week, with an advance of 1s. a week in the following years till the expiry of his apprenticeship.' Young Cook refused these terms, and, at the end of the six-months' trial, returned to his father's Leicester office.

There he preferred to use his great muscular strength at the press rather than set type. It is said that he could work off more posters within a given time than any journeyman printer when, in those days of the hand-press, the job was considered the hardest kind of indoor exercise. At the busiest times, he would perform prodigious feats. 'He would sometimes begin work at six or seven o'clock on a summer's evening, with a double-royal Columbian press, and throw off as many as two thousand double-royal* posters before breakfast-time the next morning, when he would leave the office, and take the train to some of the large towns in the Midlands with these posters, and see them exhibited on the walls before he left. This was not an exceptional performance; on the contrary, it was frequently repeated night after night and day after day during the busy season. Mr. J. M. Cook is able to boast that, when excursions by rail were novelties, there was not a market town of any consequence between Rugby in the south, Bristol in the West, Bradford in the north, and Lowestoft in the east in which he had not distributed his own hand-bills and announcements of excursion trains, while the billposter was simultaneously covering the walls with notices.'

By the winter of 1850-1, when, between seasons, Thomas Cook, influenced by Buckingham, had 'nearly settled terms for a Tour to America,' father and son shared an unrivalled experience in arranging excursions and in dealing with the problems which arose from the new industry they were creating. An overriding call was about

* i.e., 30 ins. by 25 ins.

to be made on this experience; which was to thrust aside
the American project. One morning, towards the close
of 1850, Thomas set out from Leicester to Liverpool,
intending to sound the shipping companies on his schemes.
He halted at Derby and there met John Ellis, M.P.,
chairman of the Midland Railway, with whom was his
friend and associate Joseph Paxton.

It was Ellis who, in the previous summer, had contrived
the opportunity for consideration of Paxton's last-minute
design for the building that was to house the Great
Exhibition of 1851. Now, while they were listening to
Cook intent on discovering America, more than two
thousand men were working in Hyde Park so that Paxton's
crystal palace might be ready against the Queen's opening
of the Exhibition on the coming May Day. But when at
last 'the blazing arch of lucid glass' should leap to meet
the sun, how were the necessary crowds from the rest of
the country to be got to London? In the light of recent
experience, the answer seemed obvious enough to the
three men gathered in Derby on that winter's morning.
It is likely that there had been previous tentative discus-
sions of programmes for excursionists to London in the
Exhibition months, although, as we know, Cook had
hitherto been allowed access only to one line for London
traffic, and that but for a mere two or three excursions a
year.

Cook's talk of America was stayed. Ellis, as Chairman of
the Midland Railway, over which Cook had first developed
his excursion arrangements, thoroughly appreciated his
capabilities and told him that he must not go to the States,
that his services would be indispensable during the
Exhibition months, in organizing and publicizing popular
excursions to London from every point in the Midland
system.

Paxton in his role of railway magnate, no doubt also
recalling earlier meetings at Chatsworth, must have been
almost as familiar as Ellis with Cook's activities. He now

added his insistence to that of Ellis. Cook capitulated. Before he left Derby, he agreed to advertise and conduct special excursion trains during the Exhibition months, from May to October. The whole of the southern part of the line was for this purpose exclusively allotted to Cook; north of Sheffield, although the chief responsibility was his, he was to work with Messrs. Cuttle and Calverly, 'occasional agents,' of Wakefield. In return for his efforts, he was to receive a commission of several shillings for every excursion passenger.

Thomas Cook was elated. The prospect to him as a business man was gratifying. But his 'warmest enthusiasm' at being drawn within the Exhibition's orbit was aroused in serving the ideals for which, in the minds of many, it was to stand. Was not this concourse of the peoples to usher in a reign of peace, when the only international rivalries would be in the fields of art and industry and commerce? It was an ideal at least that Cook could gladly serve; not less as because his instrument of service was the railway which clearly was steaming towards the millennium. Charles Mackay, now chiefly remembered, if at all, as the father of an illegitimate daughter, Marie Corelli, crystallized the enthusiastic moment in such lines as these:

'Lay down your rails, ye nations, near and far;
Yoke your full trains to Steam's triumphal car;
Link town to town, and in these iron bands
Unite the strange and oft-embattled lands.
Peace and improvement round each train shall soar,
And knowledge light the ignorance of yore.
Men, joined in amity, shall wonder long
That Hate had power to lead their fathers wrong;
Or that false glory lured their hearts astray,
And made it virtuous and sublime to stay.
Blessings on Science and her handmaid Steam;
They make Utopia only half a dream.'

The Exhibition project also appealed to Cook the abstainer. Invitations to tender for the catering stipulated that the refreshment rooms must not 'assume the character of a tavern.' To that end, no intoxicants were to be permitted, and the consumers of 'light and moderate refreshments' were not to be allowed to sit. The ideals of temperance were served. In fact, the hungry and the thirsty at the Exhibition stood and washed down nearly two million buns with more than a million bottles of non-intoxicants. Order was soberly maintained: one of the very few disturbances occurred when three women were violently assaulted by a party of Welsh abstainers.

CHAPTER ELEVEN

The Great Exhibition and After

THE Great Exhibition was conceived not only to show all nations the wonders of newly-industrialized Britain, but to let British workers marvel also. This meant the organization of massive pilgrimages that were themselves a novelty, in a world where so many of the workers were still tied to the land. The moment the novelty was realized, competition followed. It was competition as relentless as only the railways—and in our own times the airlines—could make it. As soon as he had signed his agreement with the Midland Railway, Cook laid about him with characteristic energy. During the three months prior to the opening of the Exhibition, he toured the principal midland and northern towns, helping to form and foster Exhibition Clubs for working men. By making small weekly payments, members qualified for transport to London and for board while staying there. This popular device may not have originated with Cook, but he was to make much use of it. Because of his experience in dealing with the accommodation, as well as the transport of large numbers of tourists, his advice was sought by the Home Office which had the job of organizing lodgings for the anticipated invasion of visitors. Cook delightedly saw in this opportunities to advance the interests of temperance hotels and boarding-houses.

It is almost certain that it was in connection with the Exhibition that Cook first founded *The Excursionist*, the publication which for long was his main general means of communication with the public, and the death of which as a casualty of the Second World War is still mourned by the faithfuls who inherited a taste for it from an earlier generation. Early numbers of *The Excursionist* defy search, but later issues bear the legend 'Established in 1851.'

At last, all was in readiness for the pilgrimage to the shrines of progress and improvement. One May Monday morning, Cook and the superintendent of passenger traffic for the Midland Railway were up to see the first Exhibition excursion train leave Leicester at five o'clock. It was satisfactorily crammed with passengers at the advertised return fare of fifteen shillings. Everything augured well. But the Great Northern line, in general competition for the London traffic, were also running excursions that day. Word got through to the Midland that their rivals had brought London return fares from Bradford, Leeds, Sheffield, and other competing points, down to five shillings. By nine o'clock that morning, the Midland had followed suit.

It was a stroke made practicable only by Cook's attitude. He knew something of competition, and he had long since realized that between the two lines it would be cut-throat. He had already advised the Midland directors that it might become necessary to carry passengers from Midland districts to London at two or three shillings each.

'But, Mr. Cook,' said John Ellis, their Chairman, 'your agreement will prevent us from doing that.'

'I have foreseen what you mention,' replied the excursionist. 'There is my agreement.'

He tore the document into pieces, throwing them into the waste-paper basket. It was the only formal legal instrument (other than a few leases and agreements for the joint occupation of branch offices) ever made between the company and himself; but its dramatic disposal was of inestimable goodwill value. Armed with the confidence of the railway directors, 'Field-Marshal' Cook threw himself into the excursion-war with happy zest.

The Exhibition time was one of tense excitement for the Cooks. John Mason, now seventeen, was his father's chief assistant throughout. The pair worked themselves harder than ever before. All trains on the Midland and the London and North Western lines, except the day express, were made available to the excursionists. The night mail was often made up of as many as six sections. Many of the special trains to and from London were run in the night, and from June until October Thomas Cook rarely slept a night at home, getting what rest he could in the trains themselves. John Mason almost lived his young life on the rails during this period. Sometimes he travelled for five consecutive days and nights, either in an excursion train loaded with passengers or in a train returning empty. He frequently travelled three or four times a week in each direction between Leeds, Bradford, Sheffield and Derby. He would leave Derby on a Friday night with trains of empty carriages bound for Leeds or Bradford. He then paraded these places in a van with a band of music, met the workers as they poured from mill and factory, per-suaded them to the trains, and accompanied them to London. Not all the 'tripper-tykes' were thrifty members of the carefully-planned Exhibition Clubs. Silver watches by the bushel went up the spout at week-ends in Leeds and Bradford to raise the five shillings for the fare, with perhaps a little pocket money.

The season closed triumphantly with Thomas Cook taking three thousand school-children from Leicester, Nottingham, and Derby to see the wonders of the Crystal Palace. The youngsters were carefully shepherded on the train and a remarkable collection of omnibuses, vans, and cabs took them and their teachers from the railway station in London to Hyde Park and back again at the day's end. Those three thousand brought up the total of Cook's

Exhibition-excursionists to 165,000, and he was thus responsible for some three per cent of the Exhibition's 6,009,948 visitors. But many of this total were Londoners and near-Londoners, who probably made a number of visits; others were from overseas. The percentage of provincial visitors under Cook's arrangements must therefore have been in fact higher.

If, after these triumphs, the Cooks returned home to Leicester somewhat exhausted, they did not allow themselves to remain inactive long. It is true that Thomas Cook's projects for exploratory visits to the Continent, the States, and the East were for the time being suspended, but plans for Scottish and other tours, abandoned in 1851 in face of the Exhibition demands, had to be resumed. The 1852 season seems to have reverted very much to the pattern of 1850.

Thomas Cook's proudest moment in 1852 was a local event, the laying of the foundation stone of the Temperance Hall in Leicester. He had gone a long way since 1841 when his modest scheme for raising a few hundreds for a similar project had lapsed. Now he and others, since a first meeting at his hotel in 1844, had raised some ten thousand pounds in 844 shares—two thousand of which was by building society loan. The Leicester Temperance Hall Company had been formed. A site fronting Granby Street had been bought, its clearance involving the demolition of nearly fifty noisome common lodging-houses. Despite pouring rain, 'the famous George Cruikshank and numerous gentlemen of the town' attended the foundation ceremony. George Cruikshank, after a riotous early life, was finally converted to total abstinence by his own designs of *The Bottle* in 1847, at which time he also gave up smoking. He spent much of his remaining thirty years as an impulsive advocate of the cause, in the interest of which he attended thousands of temperance meetings. He made a drawing of the foundation scene in Leicester in which Thomas Cook was shown sheltering beneath an umbrella.

Gradually, during the next twelve months, the building rose, Corinthian-pillared and pedimented, no mean addition to Leicester's amenities. It was temporarily opened at Whitsuntide, 1853, but was not in full use until October of that year. Its ramifications were subsequently described in a local guide book: 'A broad corridor leads to the various parts; these are a large hall, 100 ft. by 58 ft., which with its galleries will seat 1,700 persons, and the floor and orchestra about 1,000; a lecture-room, 45 ft. by 35 ft., which will accommodate about 350; library, committee, and two other large rooms. . . . Its fine organ adds much to its success.' It was of course mainly intended for the Temperance Society's use, but was generally available. 'The Temperance Hall,' we are told, 'has probably seen more exciting scenes than any other building in Leicester, with the exception of the Castle.' When Jenny Lind, the Swedish Nightingale, sang there in 1856, the takings were more than £1,000. Another throng filled the place, in 1872, to hear the Tichborne Claimant attempt to make out his case. The shell at least still stands, much as it was, although long divorced from its first uses. It was a theatre for a while. It is now a cinema.

Prompted by its architect, James Medland of Gloucester, Thomas Cook decided to build on his own account. Very soon, therefore, the Hall, regrettably flanked on one side by the 'Nag's Head,' was more satisfactorily supported on the other by 'Cook's Commercial & Family Temperance Hotel,' 63, Granby Street, a venture which cost its proprietor £3,500 to open. His move to new and larger hotel premises was undoubtedly well-advised, whatever the source of his capital. As we have seen, many of his excursionists in the summer months had, willy-nilly, to put up in Leicester overnight; and commercial accommodation must have been increasingly inadequate in a place developing probably more rapidly than any other in Britain. The population of 17,000 in Cook's boyhood was to become 140,000 before his death.

He proudly advertised his new house: 'This new and beautiful edifice ... with adaptation to the special character of hotel business ... comprises commercial-room, dining-room, coffee-room, sitting-rooms, and numerous bed-rooms, all newly furnished in style corresponding with the general appearance of the house.' It was, of course, conducted on strict temperance principles; but, in safeguarding the comfort of those like-minded with himself, Cook made to those who enjoyed 'the filthy atmosphere of smokeries,' a slight concession. He advertised that 'arrangements are made by which those to whom Tobacco-smoking may be offensive are free from the annoyance, a Room being appropriate to the use of smokers.' The shell of this building, long since converted into shop premises, also still stands.

Cook was invited to turn his attention to Ireland before the opening of the Dublin Exhibition in May, 1853. The expressed purpose of the Exhibition was to display works of industry 'by way of encouragement and example' to the Irish; but it was hoped that visitors to Dublin might go on to tour the country. Such beauty spots as Killarney were already well known. With this in view, C. P. Roney, described by Cook himself as 'the founder of the Irish Tourist Ticket system,' sent for Cook to work out plans for a double system of excursion and tourist arrangements. This perhaps calls for a momentary digression on language. The words 'excursion' and 'tour' have already been much used in this book, I hope in a sufficiently Cookian sense. Thomas Cook's own differentiation is: The term EXCURSION is generally used to designate a special trip, or trips, at very reduced prices, and under extraordinary arrangements ... whilst the word TOUR takes a wider and more circuitous range, and provides the means of travelling at special rates, and by a more organized system, but taking the regular modes of conveyance.'

Roney's ideas for Ireland combined the two. Cheap excursions were to be worked by special trains, and a fortnight was to be allowed on the tickets. The tourist tickets were to be good for all trains, and valid for a month, at rates nearly double those of the excursions. 'I was to undertake the excursion department,' Cook wrote afterwards, 'whilst the various railway companies of England would take charge of the issue of tourist tickets with the view of encouraging travel in Ireland. I was to be able to give my travellers tickets for Cork, the Lakes of Killarney, Connemara, etc., at greatly reduced prices, and the famous Mr. Dargan, the Fishbournes, and others, placed their cars* at my disposal. Thus was inaugurated the tourist system of Ireland, which with certain modifications and extensions, has continued to this day.'

While the Dublin Exhibition was running, Cook organized weekly or fortnightly excursions to Ireland from the Eastern, Midland and Staffordshire districts. He was not the only English agent to collaborate with Roney; he himself mentions others working on a similar basis from the West of England. For a while, after the Exhibition, his Irish excursions, first undertaken in 1848, were allowed to lapse; but somewhat later he was to include all the principal Irish lines in his arrangements and, further, to attract by reduced fares, such travellers from the Continent and America as wished to leave vessels at Queenstown to indulge in Irish sightseeing before crossing to England or Scotland.

It was not really until 1854 that Cook was back in his stride with his routine programme which the 1851 Exhibition had interrupted. Enlargement of this and the exploration of all the wonderful travel potential outside the British Isles seem to have been shelved for the time being, although more than a decade's experience must have suggested to the Cooks that the business of travel might profitably become their main preoccupation. Yet the progress of Cook to date as excursion and tourist agent was almost wholly adventitious. The business was not only

* Of course, the light two-wheeled Irish jaunting cars.

seasonal, but depended upon arrangements with the railway companies which were made on an annual basis. There could be no long-term policy. As the railways merged into larger amalgamations, their business was becoming more stereotyped. There was less latitude for outside individual enterprise than in the more informal days of the numerous smaller lines. Moreover, the success of such agents as Cook brought home to railway directors the importance of excursion traffic. Railway companies were beginning to appoint their own excursion managers.

The most likely scope for the expansion of an agency such as Cook's was in foreign travel. After the event that seems clear enough, though for Cook who may well have grown to manhood without ever meeting a fellow-countryman who had been abroad, there were many qualms. Such a venture, moreover, needed capital, which Cook at this moment lacked. The returns from the travel agency must have been modest enough since they could not provide for the full-time employment of John Mason Cook. The building and equipment of the Temperance Hotel had involved a considerable outlay which would take some time to recover. The printing business was falling away.

Thomas Cook's career as a general printer and publisher, indeed, came to an end in 1854. The reasons for this are obscure. Some brief notices of his life state that he had incurred heavy losses. His own explanation, much later, was that 'I found it necessary . . . to dispose of the printing office, and to devote myself more exclusively to tourist operations.' Yet a vast amount of print must have been used in publicizing these tourist operations and in the prolification of handbooks which went with them. Surviving specimens of these latter continue for some years to employ the imprint: 'Printed and published by T. Cook . . .' It is thus possible that Cook disposed of the goodwill in his general printing work but retained sufficient plant for the needs of his tourist agency.

The tale of 1854 closes with the death of Mrs. Smithard, the mother of Thomas Cook, in her sixty-fourth year. She was buried in the Baptist graveyard at Melbourne, near her first husband, John Cook. If her eldest son, in his mid-forties at the time of her death, had not yet attained a destined prominence in the great world, he was nevertheless a figure of significance in his immediate sphere and a recognized leader in most local activities for social better-ment. Mrs. Smithard, towards her life's end, must have dwelt with loving pride on the progress of the once penny-a-day garden-lad in pursuit of an ideal of service which she, to the best of her unlettered abilities, had helped to inculcate in the days of his Melbourne childhood.

─────── **CHAPTER TWELVE** ───────

First Steps Abroad

IT was the Paris Exhibition, in the year following his
mother's death, that finally sent the hesitant ambitions
of Thomas Cook outside the British Isles—to encounter
for the first time, as one whose perfunctory schooling
certainly included no languages, the mysteries of a foreign
tongue. It was too late in life to study grammar, though
not too late to girdle the globe so that the proud boast could
be made in later years: '. . . I carried my Temperance
Flag pure and unsullied Round the World, never feeling
that there was an occasion for me to deviate from the
practice which I had invariably pursued at home and in
neighbouring countries.'

When, in May, 1855, the Exhibition in the Champs
Elysées was opened in state by the Emperor and Empress,
Napoleon III, despite the war in the Crimea, expressed
his hope that the building might be a Temple of Concord.
The ideal of international peace never failed to appeal
to Thomas Cook, and the present business opportunity
was in any case obvious. He tried hard to persuade the
companies controlling cross-Channel traffic to give him
facilities to work either with or for them carrying visitors
to the Exhibition. In general, they refused. The best that
Cook was allowed to do was to provide 'a trip to France,'
from Leicester to Calais, at a return fare of thirty-one

shillings. His only other cheap facility for Continental travel at this time was by the Great Eastern route *via* Harwich to Antwerp and thence up the Rhine to Cologne and Mayence. Cook could only have considered these tentative beginnings of Continental traffic as incidental to his main business within the British Isles. For some years his letter-heading continued to read: '*English, Scotch, Irish & North Wales Excursion Office.*'

Nor could the business have made any considerable profit as yet. Thomas Cook employed but one assistant, his former printing apprentice, J. R. Poyner, and his son continued to help him at intervals in the season as required, probably otherwise working as a printer. There was evidently not enough in the excursion office to warrant the full-time employment of the young and energetic John Mason Cook, even if prospects had been assured. The backbone of the business still remained the Scottish tours and the Scottish railway companies were already attempting to oust Cook and run their own excursions and tours according to the pattern he had created. It is not surprising then that in 1856 John Mason should have considered an invitation to serve the Midland Railway Company. His worth, in the light of his experience as an excursionist, apart from his personal qualities, was obvious. He had shared many of his father's responsibilities for twelve of his twenty-two years. He had grown up in the railway era. The interest and excitement of railway development had claimed much of the almost fanatic energy he had derived from his father. The energies of Thomas, partly by accident of circumstance, were dispersed over a variety of causes, sometimes, one feels, to the detriment of business. Those of John Mason, after his early experience as a printer, were almost entirely focused on the business of travel, and all else was subordinated to that.

How early he had acquired a detailed knowledge of the British railway systems is shown by the fact, quoted by Fraser Rae, that when he was fifteen 'he was sent to London by Mr. Charles Mills, then Superintendent of the Midland Railway, with a letter to the superintendent of the Eastern Counties Railway, informing him that the bearer had been despatched to supervise the arrangement of the train and the luggage which was to leave the old Bishopsgate Station on the following morning for Scotland, by way of Peterborough and Syston on the Midland Railway to Leicester and Derby, and thence by the North Midland to York, Newcastle, and Berwick. Mr. Mills stated in his letter that, though the bearer was young, yet he was the only person known to him who was acquainted with all the junctions, and who could tell the guards how to arrange for the passengers and their luggage being put down at the proper places.'

It was seven years after this incident that John Ellis, Chairman of the Midland Railway, invited John Mason Cook to become acting superintendent of that line's excursion traffic. The younger Cook, at first reluctant to become the servant of a railway company, nevertheless accepted and continued in the appointment for three years. His job was to plan and supervise all the Midland excursion traffic. He was thus required to ascertain which places and what events might justify the running of excursion trains, to submit plans for these, together with estimates of fares and schedules of times. When these had been approved, posters, handbills and newspaper advertisements had to be prepared. The audit department required instructions as to the issue of tickets. The necessary documents had to be copied and submitted in order to secure the remission of Government duty on the excursion trains. The locomotive and engineers' departments had to be advised, and instructions given for marshalling the trains and providing guards. And, as if that did not involve paper-work enough, the youthful superintendent had to fill up the forms sent to each signalman and gatekeeper on the line, warning them as to the time at which the particular train would pass his box or gate.

It could be suggested that the provision of a clerk would have economically saved much of the Superintendent's time. As it was, the volume of work was such that, during the summer season, John Mason Cook was often at his office well into the night. He was also frequently seen at those stations where traffic was heaviest, directing the movements of trains and passengers. Fraser Rae writes that his diary shows that 'during the three years he filled this position . . . the average number of his hours of labour during the summer months was eighteen out of the twenty-four.'*

During the winter John Mason prepared statistics and checked the Clearing House excursion returns, travelled over the system investigating claims and staff irregularities, and assisted generally in the work of the Superintendent's department. His reward for so much was to be assessed in terms of experience rather than of cash. He gained a valuable mastery of all the details of management of an English railway, but at that period of low railway salaries, his rate of pay was but £75 a year. Not all his time, however, was given to the Midland Railway. He had stipulated at the outset that he should be free to help his father when he could do so without detriment to his official duties, and he thus remained in close association with Thomas, who doubtless reaped some advantage from his son's official position.

The year of his son's taking service with the Midland Railway, 1856, was generally one of expansion and development for Thomas Cook. He advertised 'a grand circular tour on the Continent' to start for Antwerp by way of Harwich on July 4th. He himself conducted the party, although he had to rely on the services of an interpreter. The party went from Antwerp to Brussels,

* The statement comes perforce at second-hand. Since Rae wrote, in 1891, the diaries of both Thomas and John Mason Cook have vanished. They are certainly no longer in the possession of either the family or the firm, except for a pocket diary kept by Thomas Cook from January 1st to April 1st, 1871, with nothing of much interest in it.

visiting, of course, the Field of Waterloo, on to Cologne, the Rhine and its borders, Mayence, Frankfort, Heidelberg, Baden-Baden, Strasbourg, and Paris, whence a return was made to London by way of Le Havre and Southampton.

So many applications had been made to join the tour that Cook set out from Harwich with a second party of fifty, on August 16th. Both tours, of course, depended on careful planning as a result of the usual exploratory journey that Cook had made. So pleased were the members of the second party that they gathered in their Heidelberg hotel to pass a formal vote of thanks to their conductor, recorded their meeting and each signed the document which was presented to Cook. More practically, it is said, they regularly continued to use Cook's services.

At one of the Continental tours of 1856, six travellers broke away from the main party for a sortie into Switzerland by themselves. They encountered considerable difficulties on their way and thus 'started in my mind,' says Cook, 'an idea of Swiss tours.' This project, however, was not to be realized for another eight years.

The small beginnings, from which the as yet unforeseen vast schemes of Continental travel were to grow, were still somewhat subsidiary to Cook's general business in which two interesting innovations were made in the same year. Cook always stressed the educative value of his excursions and tours. Snippets of information about the scenery through which the excursionists, with their potential romances, passed, and the places at which they halted, were given in the handbooks assiduously compiled for each occasion and were reiterated vocally by the conductor of the affair. Doubtless children by the score had accompanied their elders on these jaunts and had guilelessly swallowed the pill of fact concealed in the jam of pleasure. Perhaps with a recollection of the proselytizing success of his previous children's temperance excursions, Cook now decided to organize special juvenile excursions, with that same pill promoted to a bolus. The first of these excursions was run in 1856 when two thousand children were carried from Newcastle to Edinburgh. There they were taken to historic places of interest and 'were brought back to Newcastle,' says Fraser Rae, with something like unction, 'filled with an amount of information which they could scarcely have obtained from any amount of school teaching.'

The second innovation made by Cook in 1856 was that of 'moonlight trips.' These were romantic too, but they were planned with great common sense in the interests of the working-classes. Trains went and returned on the moonlight nights of the summer months from the principal Midland and Northern towns to Scarborough and other seaside places, the trippers being able to spend a day by the sea without interfering with their working hours and the fares being the lowest practicable.

There were, however, others whose indigence precluded even the modest pleasures of a moonlight trip. In honour of Temperance, Thomas Cook now took part in schemes to alleviate the lot of such as dragged out their poverty in his own town of Leicester. During the spring of 1856, thousands of Leicester poor were in dire distress. A public subscription was opened on their behalf and upwards of £500 was raised, which the Committee decided should be spent in providing the ingredients for soup. It was characteristic of his practical nature that Cook undertook to carry out the scheme. He bought the materials and had them conveyed to a soup-kitchen. There, at night-times, he superintended the preparation of nearly 15,000 gallons of 'very strong superior soup' (the economist will note that the soup was prepared at a cost of a penny a pint) which, early in the morning, thrice a week, was distributed throughout the town from huge cans conveyed on carts.

Nor was this the only activity of the sort in which Thomas Cook was engaged. During a local potato famine he got the support of 'a number of gentlemen' and went into Northamptonshire where he bought several boatloads of potatoes, brought them to 'the part of the borough near the River Soar,' and then sold them in small quantities at cost-price. This was the prelude to a bigger transaction of the same kind. In 1858, the Leicester potato crop failed again, and scarcely a sound potato was to be found in the neighbourhood. Thereupon Cook went up to Scotland, bought a total of two hundred and fifty tons of sound Regent potatoes in various districts and brought them to Leicester where, the former soup-kitchen converted into a potato-store, he retailed them to the poor at cost.

The tale of Thomas Cook the progressive reformer has a little outrun that of Cook the excursion agent whom we left at the close of the season of 1856. The following year would seem to have been much as its predecessors, save for six summer weeks of furious activity on behalf of the Exhibition of Art Treasures at Manchester. This Exhibition, opened by the Prince Consort, May 5th, 1851, was, according to *The Times*, the greatest resort of visitors in the kingdom through the summer. When it closed, October 5th, it had been seen by 1,335,000 people, and the receipts totalled £100,000. Nevertheless the attendance during the first weeks was very small and the visitors were mostly local people. The Committee seem to have panicked somewhat and sent the Chief Commissioner of the Exhibition to try to come to terms with Thomas Cook at Leicester in developing a series of excursions. Both Cook and his son were in Scotland. The Commissioner, hotfoot, caught up with them at Oban. He pressed for Cook's assistance in making arrangements 'from Scotland and the North of England, from which points but little had been done for the Exhibition. Aided by the powerful influence of the president and others of the Board of Commissioners, I instantly went to work, submitted my plans to the Scotch companies, to the Lancaster and Carlisle, and to the North-Eastern. The canny Scot who commanded the chief route told me it was all in vain. I could not move the Scotch people, as it was evident that they cared but little about the Manchester Exhibition. They had advertised the country and only got thirty passengers for a special train. I pleaded hard for a few concessions in fares and travelling arrangements, but they were only granted on condition that I gave a guarantee of £250 per train. That condition I accepted for each of the four weekly excursions, the first of which yielded an aggregate of £500, and for each of the other three I covered my guarantee, exclusive of large additions from other contributory lines. . . . But my chief success was amongst my old friends of the North-Eastern. Cheap day-trips were arranged, and each day might be extended to twenty-four hours. The moon was approaching the full, and I was moonstricken, and advertised a "moonlight trip to the Manchester Exhibition." The neighbourhood of Newcastle caught the infection, and by the light of the moon we filled eighty large carriages on the first night and had to follow up the trip by a succession. By the next moon we tried Scarborough, Malton, and other distant places, and on the first night from ninety to one hundred carriages were filled and we had to wait for carriages and locomotives for several hours, and our trouble was in the multitude of passengers.

'Success all round crowned the moonlight notion, and altogether in six weeks I took 26,000 visitors to the Exhibition, and it was a singular coincidence that the last 26,000 shillings saved the Exhibition from loss,* and I was presented with a silver snuff-box in acknowledgment of my services.' An innocent presentation this for the quondam proprietor and editor of *The Anti-Smoker* who associated snuff with tobacco, opium, and cigars as intoxicating agents.

No more sporadic attempts at Continental travel appear to have been made during the remaining three years of

---

* Cook's seeming implication that his excursions just saved the day is barely warranted. The accounts show the expenditure of the Exhibition to have exceeded income by £4,000, although this was allowed to be offset as the estimated value of the Exhibition building.

the second decade of Cook's concern with the business of travel. Most of what remains to be noticed in that period is briefly told in his own retrospect of these years. After establishing the four Exhibitions—the Great Exhibition of 1851, the Dublin Exhibition of 1853, the Paris Exhibition of 1855, and the Manchester Fine Art Exhibition of 1857—as the chief of the local stimuli to travel in these years, he continues 'during this term I established a system of very popular excursions, to and fro between John o' Groats and the Land's End, with frequent extensions to the Scilly Isles. From Scilly, and from Cornwall, Devon, Somerset, and all points west, I booked passengers through to all parts of Scotland and *vice versa*. I even got at London by a sort of back door, booking passengers for Scotland from Bishopsgate, and carrying them *via* Cambridge, Peterborough, etc., to Leicester, there uniting them with Midland passengers, when I was forbidden to bring them over the direct route in connection with the Midland system. In the ninth year of this decade, some of the Scotch companies attempted to cut me out of the best part of the field, by establishing systems of tours on models that I had provided for them, but before the close of the ten years, after spending most of their tourist receipts in advertising, they agreed to give all over to my management on their behalf, and I closed the decade by the inauguration of a new and greatly extended system on an extensive basis.'

Meanwhile John Mason Cook had terminated his appointment with the Midland Railway. From his three years' service he must have gained in experience all that the job could yield, and he could not remain satisfied indefinitely with the salary of £75. Probably, too, his decision was influenced by the fact that Thomas must have had an increasing need of his help, at least in the busy summer months. Therefore, in 1859, he decided to set up in business as a printer on his own account at Leicester, holding himself free to help his father as required, and was thus engaged for the next five years.

The father continued of course to serve the cause of
Temperance whenever he could. In 1859, on behalf of the
Irish Temperance League, he helped to spread a temperance interest in Northern Ireland, by organizing a number
of excursions, for both adults and children, from Belfast to
surrounding towns in May, August and September of that
year.

Thomas Cook's confidence at the close of 1860 in
the fortune of his enterprise was justified at least by the
enhanced prosperity of his Scottish arrangements. He
had, for the nonce, freedom of action over most of the railways, steamboats and coach lines of the country, and 'for
Scotland, 1861 was a splendid year.'

He was less fortunate that year in an overseas venture.
A London Committee, under the chairmanship of Sir
Joseph Paxton, had been formed to promote a working-
men's demonstration in Paris at Whitsuntide. Cook's
co-operation was sought and he undertook to work the
country in the Northern and Midland Districts and to
make all the arrangements at his own risk. A total of 1,673
passengers was registered, 825 of these from country
districts. But not all the reservations were taken up.
Between fifteen and sixteen hundred travellers enjoyed a
successful demonstration. But Thomas Cook was compelled
to write the venture off as 'a labour of love minus profit.'
It was even less satisfactory than that. For he had to
face a loss of £120, due in part to over-heavy advertising
expenses, but more, he felt, to the terms exacted by the
South Eastern Railway Company. If these were hard in
1861, they became harsh in 1862 when Cook repeated the
idea, again at Whitsuntide and again without success.
But what Cook considered the Railway Company's lack
of equitable spirit redounded to its considerable dis-
advantage. Thereafter, for more than thirty years, he and
his firm acted in concert with its rivals.

The father continued of course to serve the cause of
Temperance whenever he could. In 1859, on behalf of the
Irish Temperance League, he helped to spread a temperance interest in Northern Ireland, by organizing a number
of excursions from Belfast to
surrounding towns in May, August and September of that
year.

Thomas Cook, towards the close of 1860 in
the fortune of his enterprise was justified at least by the
enhanced prosperity of his Scottish arrangements. He
had, for the nonce, freedom of action over most of the railways, steamboats and coach lines of the country, and 'for
Scotland, 1861 was a splendid year.'

■ CHAPTER THIRTEEN ■

A Traffic in Beds

RAILWAY exactions were not the sole reason for lack
of support for Cook's failure on the Continent in
1862. That year, of course, was the year of the
International Exhibition which, from May till November,
attracted to Brompton crowds as great as those which had
thronged Hyde Park in 1851.* All projects for excursions
and tours in that year had perforce to face the competition
of the metropolitan attraction. Even if he had had a
similar share in the Exhibition excursion traffic to that he
had enjoyed in 1851, it might well have been a difficult
year for Cook. As it was, the Midland and the Great
Northern Railways, which he usually served, decided to
dispense with any agency and to keep the Exhibition
excursion traffic under their own management. So it was
possible disaster rather than mere difficulty with which
Cook was faced had not his easy adaptability found a way
out.

It will be recalled that in 1851 Cook, although primarily
concerned with the transport of visitors to the Exhibition,
had been one of those called in to advise the Government
about housing them. He had, moreover, served as the
travelling secretary of a national demonstration temper-

---

* The comparative figures are: 1851, May 1st to October 11th, 6,009,948;
1862, May 1st to November 1st, 6,117,450.

ance committee, not only undertaking to arrange the
railway journeys of teetotallers from the provinces, but
also their accommodation in London. Thus he had
brought much business to the temperance hotels and
boarding-houses. The Exhibition of 1862 was to be as
rigidly teetotal as that of 1851. Anticipating the influx of
temperance supporters, Thomas Cook therefore decided
to provide the beds.

He discovered that a Mr. Freake was building blocks of
tenements in the middle of a large garden on the Fulham
Road, opposite Pelham Crescent, for working-class occupation. It was the kind of project to stir his idealism at any
time. Now it moved practical impulses. Each block
contained a total of a hundred rooms, divided into
separate tenements of two or three rooms, with a large
general purposes hall and other amenities as well as 'all
suitable offices.' It is perhaps of interest that the plans of
the separate tenements were based to some extent on those
of the model cottages designed under the influence of the
Prince Consort for erection in Hyde Park in 1851, and
re-erected and still to be seen as lodges to Kennington Park.

In *The Excursionist* for April 8th, 1862, Cook was able to
announce that he had taken the first of these tenement
blocks for the Exhibition season as 'being convenient for
Exhibition Clubs, Family parties and for Visitors of both
Sexes.' He advertised that 'Relations or Friends, in Parties
of two to six persons, may have a Tenement to themselves.
. . . There are large cupboards in each Tenement, for
storing Carpet Bags, etc.' Nor were large cupboards the
only inducement that Cook could offer in those days of
the ubiquitous bug (said to have been introduced into
London with timber used in the rebuilding after the Great
Fire of 1666). It was much that he could state that 'as they
(the premises) have not yet been occupied, they are
perfectly clean, and will be furnished with all entirely new
furniture.'

Cook's charges were modest enough. Bed and a 'plain,

substantial breakfast' cost two shillings, but the visitor was warned, 'The beds are designed for two persons, and if occupied by one only, 6d. extra will be charged.' The large hall had been converted into a General Refreshment Room where food might be had throughout the day. There was a charge of threepence a day for service.

The proprietor was expectedly adamant on one score. One of his regulations read: 'The Establishment will be conducted on Temperance principles, and no one in a state of intoxication will be admitted, to the annoyance of other guests.' If the punctuation is a little ambiguous, the intention is clear enough. He was, however, prepared to give way a little on the question of smoking. A large room over the kitchen was appropriated 'to the use of those who fancied they could not exist without a little smoke.' But it was the only part of the establishment in which smoking was allowed.

Cook anticipated by a day the opening of the Exhibition itself. On Wednesday, April 30th, 1862, his own premises were opened by a public temperance meeting over which the Rev. W. W. Robinson presided. The Chelsea Drum and Fife Band tapped and shrilled 'various airs' before and after the meeting at which Cook and others spoke. Cook reviewed 'at considerable length' his arrangements in 1851 and described his present plans, which included the free use of the hall for holding non-sectarian religious services on Sunday afternoons. At the close of the meeting a large flag, on which was painted 'Exhibition Visitors' Home,' was run up over the Refreshment Hall.

Soon there was no doubt as to the success of the new enterprise. Cook's ninety or so beds could not meet demands and he took over the adjacent tenement block. Nor did this suffice. The Refreshment Hall by day became a dormitory by night when another hundred beds were put down. Still the working-class excursionists came and Cook was compelled to run up a temporary annexe in front of the hall. By the close of the season, he had provided accommodation for twenty thousand visitors, many of whom stayed for more than one night.

Cook's notion made its appeal to philanthropic Victorian masters, many of whom brought or sent parties of their workpeople to visit the Exhibition and to stay under Cook's roof. W. E. Forster, who brought a party of five hundred and forty from his Bradford works, told Cook that but for his provision and its temperance character he dared not have brought so large a party to London. Another party of three hundred from the Huddersfield works of John Brooks & Sons stayed at the Visitors' Home for two nights in July. Other large parties mentioned by Cook came from Messrs. Fry & Sons, chocolate manufactory at Bristol, from the West Retford collieries and from Messrs. Albright and Wilson's chemical works at Old Bury, near Birmingham. Languages mingled as well as accents. Parties from abroad, including official delegations from Paris, Toulouse, and elsewhere, made use of Cook's accommodation. Sixty-five Germans from Mecklenburgh put up at the Homes for a fortnight, and forty Italians from Turin stayed there for forty days.

Although the railway companies had found no use for Cook's services as agent at Exhibition time, their relations with him continued friendly. *The Excursionist*, whose title was enlarged during the Exhibition months to *Cook's Excursionist & International Exhibition & Bazaar Advertiser*, carried announcements of the Midland and Great Northern excursions to the Exhibition, and these railways on all their bills advertised the Exhibition Visitors' Home and other accommodation of Cook's. Moreover, by June 2nd, Cook was advertising combined hotel and rail arrangements whereby visitors from Leicester or Nottingham might make the return journey and enjoy reserved accommodation for three nights at the Visitors' Home (bed, breakfast, tea, attendance, etc.) at inclusive charges of fifteen or sixteen shillings, and could prolong their visit at an extra cost of three shillings a day.

Cook's one disappointment was the failure of the Sunday afternoon services, due in part to lack of preachers, but mostly to absence of congregation. Most of his visitors preferred to take the opportunity of attending famous places of worship and hearing the fashionable preachers. He therefore extended the use of the hall to 'agents of the Peace Society, the Bible Society, and other Social and Christian organizations,' and also, it seems, to certain wider aspects of pseudo-science. *The Excursionist* announced 'three lectures on Phrenology and Physiology,' to be given, on May 29th, 30th and 31st, by Messrs. Fowler and Wells from New York. 'Professor' Fowler and his wife eventually took premises in the Cook building at Ludgate Circus, and these, familiar to many generations of Fleet Street, were in the occupation of their successors until comparatively recently.

At the Visitors' Home, Cook also erected a platform in the centre of the court between the two blocks of tenements and made this similarly available for open-air meetings. This platform was first occupied by a deputation from the International Temperance Convention, on September 2nd. At this time Cook was putting out feelers, hoping for a permanent identification of the buildings with the cause as Temperance Homes. But nothing came of this, and at the close of Cook's tenancy the buildings reverted to the purpose for which they had been planned.

When planning this Exhibition enterprise, Cook had not overlooked the fact that its visitors would be drawn from all classes. As well as providing for the working-classes in his Homes, he therefore undertook to cater for a 'select class of visitors' in the various 'furnished residences of private families' which he took for the Exhibition season. The first advertisement of the Visitors' Home, in *The Excursionist* for April 8th, also announced a 'Select Boarding and Lodging House, at No. 23 Ovington-square' for those willing to pay six shillings a day for bed, breakfast and tea (both 'substantial Meals with Meats,' use of a public drawing-room, and attendance). Dinners were not to be provided as a rule, but could be had. By July, Cook was advertising five such 'First Class Houses' in Ovington Square, Pelham Crescent, Pelham Place, and Sydney Place, 'all conducted under the immediate direction and control of Mrs. and Miss Cook,' and there may have been others.

It was not permitted to sell exhibits in the Exhibition. An International Bazaar was therefore established in the Exhibition Road, almost immediately opposite the main entrance to the Exhibition. Here Cook set up an office for the issue of Scottish Tourist Tickets and in connection with this, organized what he styled a Scotch Court, for the exhibition and sale on commission of Scottish productions. Here were to be seen unforgettable Scotch souvenirs in pebble jewellery or tartan woodwork; textiles and fabrics, including tartans and the Scotch tweeds of Messrs. Cook and Davidson of Aberdeen, who also displayed 'The Excursionist' Tweed Suit at forty-five shillings; Edinburgh rock and shortbread, with other confectionery and biscuits, books, maps, and music from the Scottish publishing houses, to which new additions were made as published; and lithographs of Scottish and other celebrities, including the Prince Consort, and Lord Macaulay and, almost certainly, Thomas Cook, whose portrait, at the request of his Edinburgh friends, had been executed 'in the first style of the art' by Messrs. Scott and Ferguson in the previous year. 'For the decoration of the Scotch Court,' we are told, 'with a view of making it thoroughly characteristic,' 'numerous fine deer's heads, antlers, etc., were displayed,' a scene which would daunt even the tartan-baronial revivalists of the present day.

When the last exhibit had gone from the Scotch Court, the flag over the Visitors' Home hauled down and the many beds dismantled, when the last select visitor had departed from the first-class houses, Cook reacted from all the excitement of the Exhibition season. Doubtless the months of hard work had been satisfactorily profitable, but the bright future was not visible. 'Beyond the present season all is in obscurity,' Cook wrote in the last issue of *The Excursionist* to appear that year. 'Our desire is to follow the leadings of Providence; to live while we live to some useful purpose, cultivating and strengthening those influences which, ripened and matured on earth, bear fruit beyond the grave.'

FOOD FOR STARVING PARIS. AN ARTIST'S IMPRESSION AT THE END OF THE FRANCO-PRUSSIAN WAR

JOHN MASON COOK, SON OF THE FOUNDER,
AND CONSOLIDATOR OF THE BUSINESS

CHAPTER FOURTEEN

A London Headquarters

THOMAS COOK had passed his fiftieth year when he penned those words placing himself, somewhat despondently, in the hands of Providence. He had already become a grandfather. John Mason Cook had married Emma Hodges of Mayfield, Leicester, in 1864, and Frank Henry Cook, the first baby of the third generation was to exemplify that Providence might lead to fortune this side of the grave. When he died in 1931, much respected as a man of culture, an art-collector, a generous supporter of good causes, a church-warden, one who had rarely missed a day from business, he left an estate of gross value £1,054,769 6s. 4d., net personalty £976,761 6s. 7d.

As the new grandfather entered that season he had described as 'all in obscurity,' he had certainly served many useful purposes; but estates of a million pounds sterling were as certainly beyond his imagining, then or in the future. The immediate cause for despondence lay in Scotland: the cause for hope, did he but know it, lay overseas. The Scottish railway managers refused to allow him to continue to issue tickets and decided to take the excursion business into their own hands. It was a major setback for Cook. He had to close his Scottish offices and turn his back on a profitable business which he had virtually created. He made his protest; but there was little

E

room for sentiment in that era of keen individualist competition. So he, the provincial possessing as yet not even an office in London, was forced to look towards the Continent of Europe for an outlet for his ever-active creative enterprise. 'He soon learned,' wrote Fraser Rae, 'that the new field was limited only by the boundaries of the habitable globe.'

Through the intervention of his potent ally Paxton, he was able to secure special facilities from the London, Brighton and South Coast Railway for passenger traffic to the Continent by way of Newhaven and Dieppe, if the Western Railway of France would fall in with the scheme. Armed with introductions, therefore, Cook made perhaps the most significant of all his journeys abroad. This first agreement with the French was the real foundation of the essentially international character of the business.

He had been an excursion expert for more than two decades, and he was quick to elaborate his arrangements. In Paris he made contracts both with hotel proprietors and with transport men. Nothing was to be left to chance, and the money side of it was keenly argued and firmly arranged. He, a God-fearing man from the Midlands, would see to it that his charges came through unscathed, unrobbed, stimulated, but not by the temptations of which he was well aware, if only at second hand. His was an idealistic as well as practical view of Paris, as expressed in *The Excursionist*: 'WHY SHOULD THE ENGLISH GO TO PARIS? There are not only general, but special reasons for such visits. England and France are very powerful neighbours, who should always live on terms of friendship. It is their mutual interest to be amicable to each other; and by peaceable and friendly union they may exert a powerful influence on the destinies of Europe and the world. The strongest bond of peace and friendship is that of the real and hearty union of the people of the two countries.

'The commercial Treaties of England and France cannot

fail to promote friendly intercourse, as well as to strengthen peaceful relations.

'We would have every class of British subjects visit Paris, that they may emulate its excellencies, and shun the vices and errors which detract from the glory of the French capital. In matters of taste and courtesy, we may learn much from Parisians; and on some questions of morality we may have right views strengthened. We would have every sober and steady Englishman go to Paris to learn how to value his Christian privileges, especially those relating to the Lord's Day, or the Weekly Rest . . . open scenes of folly of every grade, on the Day of Rest, require an aggregate of labour hostile to the rights of humanity, and sickening to the sensibilities of Christianity. Give us a quiet Highland Sabbath . . . in preference to the triviality, mirth and labour of a continental Sunday.'

Later he offered advice which was quite specific: 'Ladies may, without impropriety, visit the best cafés, or sit at the tables outside. Ladies should, however, on no account enter the cafés on the north side of the Boulevards, between the Grand Opera and the Rue St. Denis.'

It is difficult to associate the character of Thomas Cook with the 'Can-Can,' but even this joyous piece of human abandon came under his notice: 'The majority of these establishments, though presenting some attraction to the visitor on account of the "fast" reputation which they formerly had, are now of the most dreary description. The "Can-Can" is danced by paid performers, and is altogether of an unnatural and forced abandon. Nine-tenths of the company consist of men, attracted by simple curiosity.'

As a start, five hundred and seventy-eight people went to spend some days in the French capital at a total cost, as they delightedly pointed out to one another, which was less than their fathers would have paid to journey by coast from London to Edinburgh. For 'good railway carriages' and first-class accommodation on the cross-Channel steamers, the excursionists paid seventeen shillings and sixpence. First-class rail and a best cabin cost ten shillings more. For board and lodging, exclusive of dinners but with free use of dining-room and attendance, the charge was eight shillings and sixpence a day. How lucky would any of the seven thousand people who at peak seasons daily cross the threshold of the Cook office by the Madeleine nowadays consider themselves to find a single luncheon at the price—but what a satisfaction must their numbers provide for the ghost of Thomas Cook as he side-steps the sellers of 'filthy pictures' who traditionally haunt the travel agency neighbourhood which he did so much to create.

That first excursion to Paris was certainly an early, if not the earliest, example of successful 'package travel.' The customers were people of modest means. They were following the example, upon a modest scale, of their so-called betters who had been accustomed to make their continental tours under the guidance of a private courier. Thomas Cook, in person at first, and later by his representatives, took the place of that private courier. Unlike the great, whose couriers, in league with hotel proprietors and others, were often of dubious honesty, his tourists, solid people (described by a contributor to one of Charles Dickens' periodicals as 'tradesmen and their wives, merchants, clerks away for a week's holiday . . . smart mechanics . . .' and a Cockney element who carried London everywhere) who knew just how much they could afford, travelled with the assurance that their journey could cost no more. They were the forerunners of the British and American families who save up to buy an all-in 'package' holiday every year.

Not content with the Paris success which so surprised his reluctant collaborators in the L. B. & S. C. Railway, Cook next went on to Switzerland. There, railway and hotel proprietors still almost innocent of their destiny to create *le playground de l'Europe*, greeted his ideas with enthusiasm. Indeed, Professor W. Hunziker, in an official record of a hundred years of Swiss tourism, refers to the forming of the British Alpine Club in the 'fifties and Cook's first 'voyage accompagne' in the 'sixties as the foundation of the Swiss tourist industry. Five hundred people responded to Cook's first advertisement of Swiss tours. The complement indeed was so large that the tour had to be run in two parts, leaving on successive days. No wonder there was a ring of triumph in what he wrote from Paris in August, 1863: 'France and Switzerland now present to me new and almost unlimited fields of tourist labour.'

On, then, to Italy—by diligence across Mont Cenis to Susa and thence to Turin, Milan, Florence and Genoa, returning by the Corniche to complete the initial personal survey. The first excursionists to Italy left England on July 4th, 1864, leaving many others disappointed; for the event was much publicized at the time and the applications many in excess of the tickets available. The great days of European excursionism were beginning. The idea had started to snowball. Railway Companies granted Cook the right to issue coupon tickets. The Swiss gave his ticket-holders a reduction of thirty per cent. What had begun as a revolution in mobility for the working-classes of the Midlands was developing into an attack upon the very insularity of the British masses—and largely because the Scottish railway bosses mistakenly assumed that they could run their own excursion business without the help of Thomas Cook. From the owners of steamboats and coaches in Scotland came stories of losses, as the railroad men, swamped by high costs and competition, realized their mistake.

The days of the Grand Tour as such were brought to an end by the Napoleonic war. Travellers thronged to the Continent after peace had been made, to Paris, either as their journey's end or merely as a first stopping-place on the way to Italy or even further afield. Of course, most were sufficiently well-off to afford their own carriage and the services of a courier, but there were humbler travellers content enough with the diligence. The development of railway travel greatly added to the number of these latter, frequently to the distaste of their more privileged compatriots.

There is some indication in *Bleak House*, written 1851-53, of how far afield the middle-classes were holidaying: 'The bar of England is scattered over the face of the earth . . . in Switzerland . . . at a French watering-place . . . roaming, with a characteristic delight in aridity and dust, about Constantinople . . . on the canals at Venice, at the second cataract of the Nile, in the baths of Germany, and sprinkled on the sea-sand all over the English coast. . . . All the young clerks . . . pine for bliss . . . at Margate, Ramsgate or Gravesend . . .'

For years before the Cookites, as they were called, invaded the Continent, there were complaints of foreign travel being spoilt by the multitude. *Household Words* which Charles Dickens 'conducted' had, as early as 1851, referred to such parties at home as 'the boon of these cheap excursions on the English railways.' The swarming of the Cookites over the Continent of Europe and the complaints which sometimes followed them, titillated the keen Dickensian journalistic nose again ten years later. In an 1864 issue of *All the Year Round*, he printed Edmund Yates' account of an interview with the new phenomenon of international travel. This interview took place in the conservatory of 'Cook's British Museum Boarding House,' 59, Great Russell Street. It was one of the old Bloomsbury dwelling-houses, since pulled down to make way for the mansion flats which now face the courtyard of the British Museum. It was admirably placed for the accommodation of excursionists in transit, but the terms of the lease forbade the carrying on of any form of trade or—lest the essential gentility of the neighbourhood be jeopardized —any show of trade signs. So the small conservatory was converted into Cook's discreetly-hidden first London office for interviews and the issue of tickets—a modest fore-

runner of the great six-storey building in Berkeley Street
where the Booking Hall alone occupies a quarter of an
acre.

Edmund Yates' article, entitled *My Excursion Agent*,
appeared in May, 1864. Thomas Cook had made it clear in
his interview that he was not a contractor who took over
the work of the railway companies, but that his own profit
came simply from a commission on the fares of those he
induced to travel—already at that time claimed to total
a million. Cook went on to explain that he did not set out
to cater for his excursionists but did his best to 'indicate'
where they could be housed and fed in comfort at a
reasonable price. If they preferred, he would settle all
hotel bills, being repaid at the end of the journey. 'It
speaks highly,' Yates reported, 'for the honesty of excursionists when Mr. Cook declares that during his whole
experience he has never made a bad debt amongst them,
or lost a farthing by them. Had he ever been asked to lend
any of them money? Frequently, and had never refused! He
had lent as much as twenty pounds to one of his excursionists, an entire stranger to him, and had been repaid.
Had he taken any security? Not he! Sometimes a gentleman would offer his watch, but what did he want with a
gentleman's watch? He told him to put it in his pocket
again.'

Edmund Yates wound up the account of his interview
with the quiet personality in the conservatory, who was
beginning to enjoy such an interesting reputation, with
this peroration: 'Now surely this kind of thing is a good
kind of thing, and ought to be encouraged. It is right that
a hard-working man, labouring in one spot for fifty weeks
in the year, should, in his fortnight's holiday, betake
himself to some place as far away from and as different to
his ordinary abode as lies within the reach of his purse, and
this he can only do by the aid of such providers as my
excursion Agent. . . . If these, then, be, as I fancy they are,
some of the results of the work of my excursion Agent—

work in itself requiring clearness of intellect and honesty and stability of purpose—I think I have a right to claim for him a position, modest but useful, in the great army of civilization which is marching throughout the world.'

It may well have been almost the last time the conservatory was used for anything so momentous. Early in the next year Cook formally set up a London office. While Leicester remained the city of his adoption, his spiritual home, Cook emerged as a national figure with headquarters very properly in the capital when he established himself at 98 Fleet Street. This position, at the corner of Bride Lane, was handy enough for the great London railway termini and equi-distant from City finance and West End fashion. It was, moreover, in the midst of the newspaper and publishing world—an appropriate setting for the beginnings of a headquarters which, though it moved west in the changing London of the 'twenties, now publishes and distributes a million and a quarter illustrated publicity brochures and folders every year.

Fleet Street beginnings were nothing if not cautious. It was considered sufficiently hazardous to have taken a whole house on lease. The upper floors, which were not required by the agency, were set apart as 'Tourist and General Boarding House, run on the familiar lines of the Bloomsbury Boarding House and the Temperance Hotel in Leicester. The ground floor was not simply an office for 'the issue of tourist tickets' but a shop for the sale of guide books and other publications and for 'the supply of tourist requisites' such as 'carpet and leather bags, hat-cases, telescopes, and Alpine slippers.' The procuring of passports—in those happier times required only for a very few countries—was an additional service offered to clients, who could also be insured through the Railway Passengers' Assurance Company. To this was added a forwarding and delivery service for parcels to all parts of the country and an advertising agency for the London and provincial papers. It was at this time that John Mason Cook became

the full-time partner of his father. Since leaving the
service of the Midland Railway, he had been in business
on his own, helping his father only in peak seasons in the
summer. His entering the partnership on a full-time basis
liberated his father, as the latter explained in a letter,
'from details of office work, and enabled me to carry out
foreign schemes of long projection in both the Eastern and
the Western hemispheres.' The establishing of that familiar
style of *Messrs. Thos. Cook & Son* marked the final change-
over of the son from a part-time to a full-time basis. The
great work which was at last to be 'limited only by the
boundaries of the habitable globe' was no longer associated
in anybody's mind with the philanthropic motives of a
provincial printer, though the principles of good work
continued to burn ardently. The establishment in Fleet
Street marked the beginnings of an enterprise which was
to be wholly professional for both men.

John Mason Cook was given charge of the London
office. His staff at first consisted of an old friend of his
father's—probably the former apprentice and general
handyman, J. R. Poyner—with a boy to act as messenger.
The new manager's tasks were arduous. He conducted the
correspondence in the intervals of attending to the needs
of the ground floor office. He became the editor of *The
Excursionist* which, in spite of the new Fleet Street address,
continued to be published in Leicester. There was so little
time to spare away from the London office on publication
day that the younger Cook would leave for Leicester on
the night before publication, returning by the mail train
in the morning.

Within less than ten years, the Fleet Street premises
proved to be too small. A quite grandiose building was
then erected in Ludgate Circus as a Central Office. When
this was first occupied in the 'seventies, it was considered
challengingly large for such an undertaking. It was a
familiar landmark to generations of travellers and of
newspapermen. In the 'eighties, indeed, John Mason Cook,

that teetotaller from birth, was so distressed by the drinking habits of Fleet Street that he founded a teetotal club for pressmen in the upper part of the building. 'He installed a Yorkshire Quaker as manager' recalled a writer in 1941, in the *Christian World* (itself produced in part of the former Cook building), 'handing over the top floor for the use of the newcomer and his eight children. My correspondent, who was number seven in the manager's family, says that two men who used the place were Irish, a young politician-journalist named T. P. O'Connor, and a certain critic with a red beard, known to-day as G. B. S.; Passmore Edwards of the old *Echo*, W. T. Stead and H. W. Nevinson were also members. Even with such ardent spirits as fellow clubmen, the journalistic fraternity failed to support this venture. The club closed its doors after three years, never having been a financial success.'

There are members of the present staff of the firm who recollect the Ludgate Circus Central Office during the reign of John Mason Cook, who matched his father both in character and energy. One, Donald White, who is said to personify 'The Man from Cook's,' and even now, in his seventies, delights to remain on duty at Victoria Station, recalls how the younger Cook, 'a very dapper little man, thickset, with a small beard,' would arrive punctually in the mornings. Before entering the office, he made a point of inspecting the outside to make sure that the posters were clean—a necessary precaution in those days of heavy horse-traffic when the mud spattered across the pavement at Ludgate Circus.

In such matters as the health of members of his staff, John Mason Cook was paternally autocratic. Donald White recalls that if any employee seemed to be 'under the weather,' he was sent peremptorily across Fleet Street to the rooms of a certain Dr. Green. If the Doctor's examination suggested that the employee was indeed ailing—and woe betide malingerers—a note would go back to John Mason Cook recommending time off for

Reproduced by permission of the proprietors of Punch

THE LUDGATE CIRCUS OFFICE AS SEEN BY *Punch* IN 1889 WITH MANY RECOGNISABLE PORTRAITS SUCH AS HENRY IRVING, ELLEN TERRY, OSCAR WILDE AND GENERAL BOOTH.

recuperation at a seaside resort. Cook's action was ruthless and thorough. He presented the employee with a return ticket for the resort intimated by the doctor, a coupon for lodging expenses, and half-a-crown pocket money. The man's full wages for his leave-of-absence period were then forwarded to his wife or his mother.

Members of the staff were obliged to put on uniform when they left Ludgate Circus for outside duty. The frock-coat which they wore then is still familiar, though the peak cap of those days—similar to that now worn by station-masters at Paddington Station—has been modified in line with contemporary military headgear. A period of great discomfort for the staff at Ludgate Circus was when the Cooks, influenced no doubt by their own travels in the East, insisted that their uniformed men should wear upon all occasions a large white sun hat similar to a topee. It was only after prolonged and embarrassed protests that this strange headgear was withdrawn.

It was not long, of course, before the Central Office at Ludgate Circus itself was outgrown and branches had to be opened in various parts of London, as well as in the provinces, forerunners of the seventy-seven branch offices throughout Britain which serve the needs of the firm to-day.

CHAPTER FIFTEEN

Discovery of America

WITH a London office established and John Mason shrewdly consolidating the business, the despondency of the earlier 'sixties were swept away and Thomas Cook was at long last free to visit America in the year the Civil War ended. It was a journey that had been in his mind for more than fifteen years, and one he would almost certainly have undertaken had it not been for the call to participate in the 1851 Exhibition.

In 1865, however, when he set about to collect introductions for America, he included not only temperance workers and ministers of religion, but politicians, railway officials and civic dignitaries. The black, leather-bound book in which he carried these across the Atlantic still survives. It contains not only the introductory letters themselves but also the names and addresses of former Midland folk who had emigrated to the States and whom he intended to look up. In the forefront of the little volume is pasted a broadsheet reprinting an announcement made by the editor of *The American Phrenological Journal*, the same S. R. Wells who, in 1862, had lectured at the Exhibition Visitors' Home. 'Visitors are coming! Americans make ready!' wrote Wells, who no doubt gratefully recalled his London platform, but who evidently had also been an excursion customer. 'Open your hearts and your houses and give them a cordial reception. Such a one as you would like to receive were you set down three thousand miles from home, among total strangers. . . . Mr. Cook is the gentleman to engineer and manage this great work. Let the press lend a hand; let our landlords and hotel-keepers make ready, and let the people everywhere receive and entertain these intelligent and enterprising European excursionists. (When in England, it was our pleasure to join one of these excursions into Scotland.)'

Cook's mission, however, was that of a business man rather than an evangelist. His propaganda was explicit and, to say the least of it, propitiatory. Before leaving, he forwarded a circular letter to the press in the United States and Canada: 'At the commencement of the great work which I have proposed to myself, in the organization of a System of Excursions and Tours betwixt Great Britain, America, and the Continent of Europe, I address myself first to you, as the leaders of public opinion on the North American Continent. In Great Britain, during the twenty-five years that I have devoted to the development of various systems of cheap travelling in every part of the United Kingdom, as well as in France, Switzerland, and Italy, my best assistants and allies have been connected with the newspaper and periodical press. Editors of, and contributors to, many of the principal journals of England and Scotland have generally regarded my work as appertaining to the great class of agencies for the advancement of Human Progress, and to their generous aid I have been indebted for much of the success which has crowned my exertions.'

Leaving no stone unturned, he penned this address to the people of America: 'In England and Scotland more than a million tourists and excursionists have availed themselves of my arrangements; tens of thousands have travelled with me, many making it a yearly practice to make a trip under my arrangements. These have been my best advertisers, inasmuch as they have recom-

mended my tours to their respective circles of friends and
neighbours. . . . The subject of excursions to America
has been repeatedly urged upon me, and but for the
disorganization of the Great Republic I should in all
probability have gone into the matter two or three years
ago. But this, after all, seems to be the best time for a great
attempt to harmonize extensive schemes of American and
European travel. My own Continental Tours have reached
a point of interest and solidity which gives me encouragement to combine with them the interests of another
Continent; and in America, too, there is now a field of
operation of unparalleled scope and interest.'

Among his letters of introduction was one from William
Edward Forster, M.P. for Bradford and at that time Under-
Secretary for the Colonies: 'I am very glad to find by your
letter of the 17th inst. that you intend arranging for
excursions between England and America during the year
1866. Such intercourse, well managed, would not only be
of advantage to the individuals travelling, but would be of
real service to both countries, by removing the prejudices
which are the results of ignorance, and which will quickly
yield to the kindly influences of mutual hospitality; and as
regards management, these excursions cannot, I am sure,
possibly be in better hands than yours.'

John Bright, M.P. for Birmingham, one of the strong
personalities to emerge from the manufacturing classes as
a force in nineteenth-century politics and incidentally an
ardent supporter of the Northern cause in the Civil War,
wrote: 'Dear Sir, I have read your circular with much
interest. Your project is one that will involve great care
and responsibility—but with your long experience, I do
not doubt its success. If you can assist some hundreds of
Englishmen to visit the United States in the course of a
year, and as many Americans to visit England, you will be
of service to both Countries. I am quite sure that much of
the unfriendly feeling which has existed here towards the
United States during the last four years has arisen from

the strange ignorance which prevailed amongst our people
on all American matters, and this ignorance, so discredit-
able and so injurious, you will do much to remove. I wish
your scheme every success—from all I have heard of you,
I feel the greatest confidence in your power to carry out
your undertaking to the satisfaction of those who confide
in you. I believe you will find in the United States a
disposition to co-operate with you, and to lessen your
difficulties in every possible way.

Another Parliamentarian who contributed to the
recommendations was Sir Samuel Morton Peto, the
contractor, who had earned a baronetcy by constructing a
railway at cost price between Balaclava and the British
entrenchments before Sebastopol during the Crimean war,
and who also constructed the Nelson Column in Trafalgar
Square in 1843, and who lived, if I may be permitted a
personal irrelevance, at Chipstead, Sevenoaks, on the very
spot where these pages are being written.

At least two American citizens, the phrenological
Fowlers, already familiar with excursion routine, added
their testimonials together with a hint of things to come:
'You are the king and father of Excursions. . . . Having
been with you to Scotland and to Switzerland, we have
found you a gentleman in every respect—gallant, polite,
good-natured and successful in planning. You understand
your business perfectly and your Phrenological develop-
ments are favourable for just such an Excursion as you
contemplate to make to America, or to Italy, Jerusalem
and round the world.'

That Cook was a prophet not without honour in his own
country, it should be added that the Mayor of Leicester
signed his letter with: 'I am, very Respectfully.' John
Bright's letter, however, was the most valuable of the
batch. 'You need no other recommendation,' he was told
on arrival, 'as the name of Bright will carry you everywhere in America.'

He set sail on his voyage of discovery in the steamer

City of Boston, a passenger vessel, incidentally, which perished without trace several years later in the Atlantic. He arrived in New York in wintry weather and had a somewhat wintry reception. The Customs authorities, to his dismay, charged him with the sum of twenty-five dollars upon the five thousand copies of the pamphlet which he had brought with him for free distribution.

Beginning late in November, he set out to tour Montreal, Toronto, Hamilton, Niagara Falls, London, Detroit, thence through the State of Michigan to Chicago. He met old friends from Leicester in the State of Wisconsin. He visited Springfield in Illinois where he saw Lincoln's house and the provisional tomb in which the President's remains had been placed. Thence by rail to Cincinnati, Philadelphia, Baltimore and Washington, to return to New York, having covered about ten thousand miles— six by steamer, four by railroad.

He found no excursion system in America comparable to that which had been growing up in Britain. He must, however, have paid a good deal of attention to the rapidly expanding enterprise of the American Express Company which already in the 'sixties maintained nearly nine hundred offices and employed fifteen hundred men. About the time of his visit, the directors of this great business that in after years was to run so often in friendly rivalry with his own, were claiming that they covered ten States with an aggregate population of over fourteen and a half millions, and were proudly offering America the slogan, 'Every man's door can be reached by this Express.' Thomas Cook, indeed, may have learnt with some envy that this Company had provided the horses and carriages when the Prince of Wales, later King Edward VII, had visited New York five years earlier and had made a glittering progress along Broadway. (His own services to Royalty were to come later.)

As early as 1858, the American Express Company, aware of the profits that had been made in arranging the passages of emigrants from Europe to the industrial areas of America where manpower was needed, had decided to try the travel business. They had accepted the agency of the Atlantic Royal Mail Steam Navigation Company, but had found that the profits were too small and it was more than fifty years before they turned again to the travel agency business on the lines that Cook was developing.

If this, his exploratory visit to America, was not the resounding success he had promised himself, Cook did at least make arrangements for special trips to be made over some four thousand miles of rail at a uniform rate of two cents, then two-thirds of a penny, a mile. It was sufficiently encouraging for the younger Cook to set out from England two months after the return of his father, in the spring of 1866, with an excursion in two parts, the first numbering thirty-five and the second somewhat less. Curiously enough, to those subjects of Queen Victoria to whom a war was so remote, one of the chief attractions in the New World was a visit to the battlefields of the South. Richmond, Virginia, and the Mammoth Cave of Kentucky were other special attractions in a journey which covered much of the territory visited by the older Cook during his exploratory visit. The daring excursionists returned home well satisfied; but not the younger Cook. He had found on arrival in New York that the railway managers refused to be bound by the arrangements they had made with his father. With characteristic energy, he at once made new ones, and these were so rapidly concluded that his charges were not held up for a single day. Of this initial disappointment, Thomas Cook wrote: 'Jealousy and competition of companies and agents defeated my purposes and destroyed my hopes. In the following winter my son again crossed the Atlantic with the view of promoting travel to the Paris Exhibition. He thought he had laid his plans securely, and several great companies promised their aid in giving effect to the arrangements, but our plans were again thwarted, after printing thousands of posters and tens of thousands of explanatory bills. The information benefited others, but left us unremunerated.'

It was the younger Cook—and it must be noted how quickly he made his business acumen felt—who finally consolidated arrangements in America. The forty-one series of tickets that Cooks would issue were to be recognized by the American railway managers, the holders of these tickets being entitled to use them when they pleased. The first Cook posters advertising American tours, offered a choice of five shipping lines. From Liverpool to New York cost twenty-five guineas return, first-class; sixteen guineas, second-class. Such was the foundation of the extensive, profitable and friendly operations which have continued in the New World to the present day.

Nor, during the long years did old Thomas Cook's pioneering spirit wane. In the reign of his grandsons, in 1927, the firm planned and carried out what is claimed to be the first escorted tour by air. This was a flight from New York to Chicago for the Dempsey-Tunney fight. There was no regular passenger air-services between the two cities at that time, so the tour was made by special chartered aircraft and the arrangements included for ringside seats for the now historic 'Battle of the Long Count.'

One of the earlier distinguished citizens of the United States to use the Cook services was President U. S. Grant. The really eloquent testimony from the New World, however, came in later years from Mark Twain: 'Cook has made travel easy and a pleasure. He will sell you a ticket to any place on the globe, or all the places, and give you all the time you need and much more besides. It provides hotels for you everywhere, if you so desire; and you cannot be overcharged, for the coupons show just how much you must pay. Cook's servants at the great stations will attend to your baggage, get you a cab, tell you how much to pay cabmen and porters, procure guides for you, and horses, donkeys, camels, bicycles, or anything else you want, and make life a comfort and satisfaction to you. Cook is your banker everywhere, and his establishment your shelter when you get caught out in the rain. His clerks will answer all the questions you ask and do it courteously. I recommend your Grace to travel on Cook's tickets; and I do this without embarrassment, for I get no commission. I do not know Cook.'

CHAPTER SIXTEEN

Golden Years

FOLLOWING the long-delayed conquest of the Atlantic came progress on an almost imperial scale. The Cooks' was a commercial empire based upon a characteristic mingling of shrewd catering for a new public taste with venturesome pioneering. The industrialization first of Britain and subsequently of other European countries together with the post-war boom in America, had created a new leisured class. The pleasures of travel were no longer limited to a privileged minority who journeyed *au prince* on the Grand Tour. For the recently-elevated middle-classes and even for the better-paid artisans, travel was an essential part of the new emancipation. Moreover, a census at the beginning of the 'sixties had shown that for the first time in Britain there was an excess of urban over rural population; and it was therefore an urge towards healthy fresh air as well as enlightenment which was making itself felt.

But the patrons of the Grand Tour had been served by couriers to smooth their progress to foreign parts and also to mitigate the extortions which lay in the path of every *milord*. How would fare their multitudinous successors, brimful of eagerness, slender of pocket, but resolute in matters of getting their money's-worth? The Cooks provided the answer. With nearly a quarter of a century's practice in handling inexperienced travellers, none was better fitted than they to meet the new need. In establishing a pattern for excursion travel in Britain, the influence of Thomas Cook upon the social life of his times had already been profound. He had been a not insignificant social emancipator in enabling the masses to enjoy the benefits of mobility. He and his son, at once moulded by the needs of the age and moulding the habits of their fellows, buoyed up by good intentions, shrewdness, and a dauntless resolve to break new ground, were ready and eager to offer themselves as couriers to the world and his wife.

There were prophets who proclaimed the new spirit Cooks so energetically canalized. Dr. James Bowling Mozley, the eminent divine, declared in a famous sermon on Nature given some thirty years after Cook's first excursion: 'The sight of nature has undoubtedly gained an extraordinary power over people's minds; witness the quantity of travelling there is, purely to get the sight of grand objects. This is rather a new feature of the world—the popular pursuit of natural beauty.'

How readily the Cooks were serving that 'popular pursuit' is indicated rather balefully by Leslie Stephen in *The Playground of Europe*, 1871, in which he refers to Swiss 'valleys which have not yet bowed the knee to Baal, in the shape of Mr. Cook and his tourists.' If the indomitable Thomas Cook had not been at hand, there would, of course, have been others to pioneer the business and take the brunt of the amused but not always amusing denigration that followed it. But it was his destiny that his name should become a household word, despised perhaps by the superior, a butt even for the sophisticated, but a veritable passport for humdrum man.

Though in most respects he was the first in the field, his enterprise was not unique. His first important rival was Henry Gaze, who set up in business as a tourist agent in 1855. It was a rivalry which seems to have been friendly enough for we find Cook advertising two of his, Gaze's, books, *The Care of the Feet* and *Switzerland: How to see it for Ten Guineas,* in a number of *The Excursionist* in 1861—and Thomas Cook's own comment upon the ten guinea business was that it couldn't be done without roughing it. Gaze began in Southampton and later set up in business in the Strand in London in the eighteen-seventies, and his firm, besides acting as shipping and money agents, conductors of tourist parties 'on land and sea' and publishers of maps, guide-books and time-tables, owned two hotels in Paris. He died in 1894.

In the latter part of the nineteenth century, other businesses started, some with origins similar to that of Cook's. There was John Frame, for instance, another fervent teetotaller who, unlike Cook, demanded strict temperance from his clients. Like Cook, he ran his first tour, in 1881, in association with a temperance demonstration—and to-day, Frames' tours are familiar to all who travel. Dean and Dawson, now associated with the Cook business, started with a factory outing from Stockport to Paris in 1871. Sir Henry Lunn began in 1892 with a special tour to Rome, and initially specialized in catering for clergymen and their families. The Polytechnic agency originated in 1872 from a holiday home at Brighton for poor members of the London Polytechnic. The American Express Company, which, as we have seen, was already a flourishing concern when Cook first visited the States, did not set up a travel department until after the start of the First World War, when, according to that Company's centenary history, 'hampered though it was by the war in Europe' it launched itself 'vigorously into the business of cruises, conducted tours, and special movements.'

In the golden years of the late 'sixties, before such rivals came upon the scene, but already tempered by long experience of keen competition and frustration, the Cooks must have looked out from the windows of Fleet Street upon a wide world bristling with opportunities. The flag of the Queen flew over a satisfactory slice of it, as

yet untroubled by anything more disturbing than local
wars. Nearly all of it offered virgin soil for the excursionist.
The only limits to the possibilities of travel were political
and physical. The economic restrictions, prohibitions and
hindrances of the Air Age were still a long way off.

At home there was a splendid new arrangement with the
Midland Railway by which Cooks were to advertise all the
cheap excursions of that Company to and from London,
combined with through bookings to all parts of the
Continent. There was a beginning of tours to the Channel
Islands. There were the first circular tours covering
Switzerland and North Italy and circular tickets from
Paris through Fontainebleau, Dijon, Macon, Geneva,
Lausanne, and Interlaken, returning by way of Strasbourg.
One of the earliest of these trips was recalled in a letter to
The Times during the 'thirties of this century by a Mr. G. F.
Young of Felixstowe.

'It was midsummer, 1868, that we found ourselves, my
sister and I, at Harwich. We had only then left school and
were to become members of a small party about to be
personally conducted on the Continent by Mr. John Cook,
son of Mr. Thomas Cook, and father of Mr. Frank
Cook, then about six years old. Mrs. John Cook, and her
mother, with two or three others in addition to ourselves,
made up the party. On arrival at Antwerp, Mr. Cook
engaged and paid for cabs for our conveyance to the Hotel
de l'Europe, M. Barber proprietor; and henceforward
Mr. Cook paid for everything—hotels, rail fares, cabs,
sightseeing Rhine boats, etc., the arrangements being that
each should pay his or her quota of the expenses on
completion of the tour, the places visited being Antwerp,
Brussels, Cologne, Bonn, and Heidelberg; and the return
via Amsterdam, The Hague and Rotterdam, and extending
to about a fortnight. This was, I believe, Mr. John Cook's
almost first experiment of personally conducting a party
on the Continent. The reason of our being of the party was
that my father was a director of the Great Western

Railway, with which company Mr. Cook wished to enter into arrangements to the advantage of both.'

The Cooks must have seen little of their London offices but much of the world during that memorable year. The son made a second stormy crossing to America where he travelled 4,000 miles, mainly by night, spending his days in interviews with railway managers in Canada and the States. He was trying to work out a system of return fare bookings between points in North America and Paris, where there was to be a great exhibition in the following year. He disseminated masses of posters and handbills, but without outstanding results. 'Some of the railway companies broke their promises and acted with advantage on the hints which they had received and did so to the detriment of those who gave them.'

Meanwhile in Italy the father was showing his mettle as a travel impresario. He was accompanying a party, fifty strong, on a trip to Rome for Holy Week and had, of course, prudently booked hotel accommodation in advance in the Eternal City. At Florence, however, a telegram awaited him from the Rome hotelier stating that, after all, not a bed was to be had, and that it would be useless to take the party any further. Cook was not one to be deterred by such crises. He telegraphed an indignant reply and rushed ahead of his party by the night train to make his personal protests, presumably through an interpreter, to the feckless hotel proprietor.

As a personal intervention this was assuredly impressive, but it failed to clear the hotel of fifty beds in Holy Week. Indignation quickly gave way to practical expediency. It is not recorded whence came the inspiration which turned the harassed Cook to palaces, but within a few hours that morning he had acquired for the sum of £500, the use of the palace of Prince Torlonia, as a lodging for his party for ten days, fixing for them to eat out at restaurants in the neighbourhood. Gratified no doubt by the unexpected splendour of their surroundings but by by no means carried

A PHILOSOPHICAL EXCURSIONIST.

Elderly Gentleman (politely to middle-aged Spinster opposite, evidently one of Cook's Tourists). "AND WHERE, MAY I ASK, ARE YOU GOING NEXT?"

Middle-aged Spinster. "OH! LET ME SEE!—I'M GOING TO GENEVA!"

Elderly Gentleman. "GOING TO GENEVA! WHY, YOU ARE IN GENEVA!"

Middle-aged Spinster. "AM I REALLY? OH, THEN I'M GOING TO MILAN!"

away by generosity, members of the party contributed £4
each towards this additional expense, thus covering half
the loss. Perhaps the gain in goodwill more than compensated for the balance.

The taste of European political stress also came his
way that year when in the autumn he led a party by way
of the Italian lakes to Venice. They arrived just as the
Austrian troops were being evacuated and stayed on to
see the triumphant arrival of King Victor Emmanuel.

Between such jaunts as these came the first direct contact
with a reigning monarch. Cook's renown as an organizer
of visitors—and their beds—for international exhibitions
evidently preceded him when he visited Paris with letters
of recommendation to make his plans for the Exhibition
of 1867. The private secretary of Napoleon III met him
with personal assurances that the Emperor was ready to
assist him in every possible way in promoting the visits of
working men from the English industrial areas to Paris.
The royal interest did not carry with it any official
appointment, but Cook was not one to be deterred by that
lack of formality. He leased open spaces at Passy, where he
ran up temporary buildings in which his excursionists
could be cheaply housed. For the reception of his first-class
visitors, he took over a large empty building at the corner
of Boulevard Haussman. The Emperor must have been
gratified by the report that arrived from Thomas Cook at
the close of the Exhibition. Twenty thousand had visited
Paris under the Cook ægis, and ten thousand of these had
slept in the beds provided by Cook.

For the period of the Exhibition, Cook acted as
Managing Agent for the London, Brighton and South
Coast Railway, the directors of which he persuaded to
issue tickets from London to Paris for 20s. return (a
century of progress in all forms of transportation has
contrived to build up this figure to a minimum of
£7 6s. 2d. (third-class) return by rail; £9 15s. 0d. by air).
The overall cost to working men spending four days in the

Paris of the Second Empire, then at the height of its glory, was 36s.

It had been a great moment for the idealist in Cook when he had participated in the great surge of working-class visitors to the Prince Consort's Exhibition in Hyde Park at the turn of the mid-century. Though his business was now clearly destined to cater more and more for the middle-classes, the spectacle of thousands of artisans from the Midlands and the North crossing the Channel, not as soldiers but as sightseers, and being accommodated at Passy cheaply and relatively free from the temptations of the City of Light, was another highlight in his life to which he loved to refer in after-years. Nor did that little master-piece of organization and improvization which had so pleased an Emperor hinder the expansion of the business at home. British excursion trains were carrying passengers holding Cook's tickets at all points between London, Penzance, Norwich and Inverness. Their smooth running had been left entirely to John Mason Cook, who had not spared himself, being out of his bed for a hundred consecutive nights while the season lasted.

To this period belongs the invention of a device upon which much of the modern system of 'packaged' or all-in travel arrangements are based, the hotel coupon. It conferred upon its bearer the right to demand lodging and meals at any hotel named within the scheme. In these days when international travel is so much more complex, there are many modifications, improvements and restrictions upon the basic principle. The new travelling public upon whose needs the Cooks founded their international business in the 'sixties were, in the eyes of most continental peoples, the lineal descendants of the old aristocracy of the Grand Tour. Like their predecessors, indeed, they may well have possessed a measure of insularity, independence, and ignorance of languages which amounted to something like arrogance. Unlike *milord*, however, they did not combine these qualities with unlimited wealth. They could not afford to be plundered. Indeed, they were the sort of people who demanded value for money's-worth and the Cook business depended upon their getting just that. Fraser Rae, writing in the 'nineties, when this was still a matter of recent history, has recorded, probably from first-hand knowledge, Thomas Cook's approach to the problem: To the Railway Companies he had already said: 'I will take tickets for particular trips at a fixed price, and I shall arrange with others to use them on my terms.' Thus the railway managers were assured of a fixed number of passengers whom Cook would induce to travel. To the hotel-keepers of the period, themselves only just becoming alive to the scope offered by the new travelling public, Cook said: 'You can afford to house and board men or women for so much a day, giving them certain rooms and repasts in return for a fixed payment. I undertake to guarantee the payment, or make it in advance, if you will enable me to arrange with the persons who visit your hotel, and claim to be lodged and entertained.' The initial effort in putting over this novel idea on a large scale must have been prodigious. The Cooks not only accomplished it, but also provided for first- and second-class travellers both on the railways and in the hotels. Cook personally tested the system on an exploratory tour through Italy to Vienna, down the Danube, through Hungary, returning by way of the Tyrol and Switzerland. When Fraser Rae wrote about the system, he was able to state that twelve hundred hotels in various parts of the globe accepted the coupons and that in these the traveller was 'free from all doubts or anxieties about the length of his bill and the accuracy of its items.'

Though these were still pioneering days, the Cook travel arrangements were nothing if not thorough. From experience gained in his own preliminary trips, Thomas Cook was lavish in his advice to prospective customers. There was an ambitious Italian tour, for instance, in 1868, which lasted a month and cost £40 a head. The party

assembled in Paris, where hotel accommodation was found
for them. Their first stop was at Chambery in the Savoy.
Thence they went to St. Michel by special train, continuing
their journey by special diligence across the Alps to Susa
where a special train took them to Turin. Then they left
by night train to Florence and were earnestly requested by
their conductor not to go on ahead of him lest their hotel
coupons should not be understood. They went to Rome,
where they spent a week, by way of Pisa and Leghorn;
thence to Naples. The prospectus of this journey offered the
customary detailed advice about luggage and personal
apparel. It included this personal, somewhat paternal note,
typical of the advice Cook loved to bestow upon his
clients: 'Nothing in former times weakened my power to
serve so much as having to contend against the eagerness
of young and active gentlemen who would run off from
the stations to secure the best rooms and to bespeak them
for others of their immediate association. I checked this
impetuosity by requesting hotel-keepers to send first-
comers, as the most vigorous, to the highest rooms; but I
more effectually repressed it by sending in advance a list
of the party, distinguishing married couples, ladies, etc.,
from others, and getting rooms allotted to all before their
arrival. It is a pity that all young and strong visitors do
not give preference to the highest rooms, which are
generally by far the most quiet and pleasant. How many
young ladies and gentlemen are there who will copy the
example of a young lady who wrote to me two years since,
requesting that I would always bespeak for her "a room
high up?" I shall be glad to receive such instructions to
note in my circular to hotels. Such preference might be
given without partiality; but if you are not prepared to
make this request, just quietly leave the matter in the
hands of myself and the hotel proprietors, and we will do
our best to make all things pleasant.'

Such confident paternalism, shared by father and son
alike, rested upon a solid foundation of negotiated business

which the Cooks constantly carried on, as it were, behind the scene, while their tourists smoothly went the rounds of Europe. John Mason Cook's diary entries over the autumn and winter of 1868-69 show that he travelled twenty thousand miles to further the passenger traffic of the Great Eastern Railway on the Harwich route to the Continent. In Germany he met opposition. The reduced fares which he proposed, they said, would take the profit out of travel. The President of the Rhenish Railway Company at first turned down his ideas as 'visionary.' Nevertheless, at a general meeting of German railway managers, the younger Cook succeeded in obtaining a trial concession. They allowed him to issue a series of special tickets on condition that he pledged himself that at least five hundred first-class passengers would buy them within twelve months. Some weeks later, Cook astonished the Germans by reporting that more than five hundred passengers had bought and used these tickets within a single month.

It is not surprising that the Cooks were among the first, and certainly among the most enthusiastic, of the admiring passengers who rode through the new Mont Cenis tunnel from France to Italy. In Europe, at least, steam was becoming all-powerful and, wherever steam drove the wheels, the name of Thomas Cook would pass into the language. Before that tunnel was blackened with use, there were passengers passing through it on Cook tickets to India and Egypt.

Yet, for all the adventure of creating their intricate pattern of excursions at home and journeys abroad, the Cooks never lost their zest for individual tasks to meet unique occasions. In the midst of his ceaseless travelling and constant negotiation, the younger Cook returned with gusto to accept an offer to act as representative of the Earl of Shrewsbury who, following the practice rather of this century than of his own, desired to throw open to the public his spacious and fantastic grounds at Alton Towers. 'There, among the hills where Staffordshire joins Derbyshire,' writes Miles Hadfield in a recent essay* on horticultural magnificence, 'everything was to be found: an imitation of Stonehenge, a copy of the ever-famous monument of Lysicrates in Athens, not a few genuine ruins and caves, an octagonal Chinese temple—all set among glades planted lavishly with exotic trees and shrubs.' Accustomed as his Lordship was to things being done on a grand scale, he must have been somewhat surprised when John Mason Cook organized a party of ten thousand excursionists to visit the property in a single day. In spite of the litter they left behind them, his Lordship was sufficiently gratified to retain the younger Cook as his representative for many more summers.

With the new European arrangements working so well, with the British Isles and much of Europe consolidated, with a third generation on the way, and the elder Mrs. Cook energetically managing the hotel businesses and pursuing nonconformist causes, it might well have seemed that father and son, men without languages or any higher education, had taken on about as much as they could handle. Yet these golden years still found them possessed with a vision 'limited only by the boundaries of the habitable globe.'

* *The Saturday Book*, *No.* 12 (Hutchinson).

CHAPTER SEVENTEEN

Denigration — and Fame

After the Dickens' investigation of the new travelling phenomena, success and fame carried the Cooks and their excursionists into the pages of *Punch*, where over the years they had a somewhat invidious attention. They were also noticed by John Close, a printer at Kirkby Stephen, who bombarded the local bigwigs with his poetasting to such effect that, with their support, in 1860, he was awarded a Civil List pension of £50. But in view of the ensuing rumpus this was commuted to a grant of £100 from the Royal Bounty. The incident did not however prick the conceit which allowed him to accept as a compliment the derisive epithet of 'poet,' and it was as 'Poet Close' that he signed such characteristic opportunisms as the verses to Cook's party: 'Poet Close's New Epic Poem in Blank Verse, respectfully dedicated to J. M. Cook, Esq., of Ludgate Circus, Fleet Street, London, E.C. Mr. Cook and his Tourists at the English Lakes on a Seven Days' Tour of a Party of the British Medical Association; when at Bowness, Windermere, they visited "The Poet Close," on August 14th, 1877:

> All hail to mighty COOK, whose clever head—
> (That *Head* devising wondrous schemes for good
> Of thousands of our Studious Men who ought to see
> The glorious landscapes and varied Scenery of

Our Native land—and breathe a purer air)—
We say, all hail to COOK, this *Philanthropic Man*,
Whose Head this Scheme to see the English lakes,
He did devise and plan . . .

But then, O COOK: new pleasures daily plans!
To ROME and over all the HOLY LAND
He takes his thousands; and to the LAKES—
A group of DOCTORS brought to-day who called—
To see the POET CLOSE and '*Interview*'
The Man whom *Punch* and all the *London Critics*—
In vain have tried to kill . . .

In the pages of *The Excursionist* Cook never hesitated to
thunder back at his critics: 'We offer to all classes and to
everybody the cheapest Tourist tickets ever presented to
the English public; and not, as some dirty fingers inscribed
in one of the Swiss Hotel Guide Books—"cheap and
nasty"—but as clean and respectable as that which such
tourists ought only to have at twice the cost. There are
purse-proud younglings who affect to treat with disdain
those who occupy a lower sphere than themselves, and
then, like a contemptuous old lady whom we once met in
the Scottish Highlands, think that places of rare interest
should be excluded from the gaze of the common people,
and be kept only for the interest of the "select" of society.
But it is too late in this day of progress to talk such
exclusive nonsense, God's earth with all its fullness and
beauty, is for the people; and railways and steamboats are
the results of the common light of science, and are for the
people also. . . . The best of men, and the noblest minds,
rejoice to see the people follow in their foretrod routes of
pleasure. . . . The immortal "Boz," in *All the Year Round*,
has very cordially recognized our efforts; the Editor of the
Civil Service Gazette has seconded the kind recognition of
Charles Dickens; and other papers are taking up the strain
of these popular journals. It has been the fashion with some
powerful papers to decry Excursions and Excursion Trains;

but a few more such articles as those to which we have referred will soon turn the tone of *The Times*, and his faithful cur, *Mister Punch*, both of whom have had silly things to say on this subject . . .'

It was following Thomas Cook's success in Italy that he sustained an open assault. It emanated from *Blackwood's Magazine* in February, 1865, the writer, a regular contributor, using his usual pseudonym, Cornelius O'Dowd. Such a pseudonym was a journalistic convention and little more, though the writer did in fact hold an appointment as Her Majesty's Vice-Consul at Spezia, and was promoted by Lord Derby (who wrote 'Here is six hundred a year for doing nothing, and you are just the man to do it') to the post of Consul at Trieste while his anti-Cook campaign was still waging. His true identity was Charles James Lever, Irish novelist and man of letters, a talented but harum-scarum expatriate who had beggared himself at the gambling tables at Baden Baden, affronted court etiquette at Karlsruhe and shocked the population of Florence by the eccentric behaviour of his family—according to the reports of Cook's protagonists. Lever's protests might have been meant merely to entertain his readers, but he certainly did not mince words. His first contribution entitled *Continental Excursionists* referred to the 'new and growing evil' of Thomas Cook having 'devised the project of conducting some forty or fifty persons, irrespective of age or sex, from London to Naples and back for a fixed sum.' He went on to describe 'the cities of Italy deluged with droves of these creatures, for they never separate, and you see them forty in number pouring along a street with their director—now in front, now at the rear, circling round them like a sheepdog —and really the process is as like herding as may be. I have already met three flocks, and anything so uncouth I never saw before, the men, mostly elderly, dreary, sad-looking; the women, somewhat younger, travel-tossed, but intensely lively, wide-awake, and facetious.'

Shortly afterwards he lightly suggested to over-credulous

Italian friends that such tourist parties included convicts whom the Government had been unable to transport to Australia. The worthy Thomas, it was implied, was really a furtive agent of the British Government. His undertaking was to loose the felons a few at a time in the various Italian cities covered by the itinerary of each tour. There is little doubt that Lever's damaging extravaganza was offered in jest; but there is no doubt whatever that there were people in Italy who took it in all seriousness and that there were prospective customers in Britain who were not encouraged.

Undaunted by protests, Lever returned to the attack in a later issue of *Blackwood's* with a piece entitled *A Light Business Requiring no Capital*. This time he referred to 'the Continental bear-leader, who conducts tribes of unlettered British over the cities of Europe, and amuses the foreigner with more of our national oddities than he would see in a residence of ten years amongst us.' He went on to rage at 'these Devil's dust tourists have spread over Europe, injuring our credit and damaging our character. Their gross ignorance is the very smallest of their sins. . . . Foreigners may say, "We desire to be able to pray in our churches, to hear in our theatres, to dine in our restaurants, but your people will not permit it." They come over, not in twos and threes, but in scores and hundreds, to stare and laugh at us. They deride our church ceremonies, they ridicule our cookery, they criticize our dress, they barbarize our language. How long are we to be patient under these endurances? Take my word for it, if these excursionists go on, nothing short of another war, and another Wellington, will ever place us where we once were in the opinion of Europe.'

There was to be war in plenty, as we all know, and between wars always a few expatriates, though rarely in official position, to deplore their country and their fellow countrymen. Thomas Cook's counter-attack, if lengthy, was resounding, as this extract shows. 'Let me ask why Mr. Lever's susceptibilities should be outraged, and his refinement trampled on, because thirty or forty Englishmen and Englishwomen find it convenient to travel in the same train, to coalesce for mutual benefit, and to sojourn for a like time in the same cities? Reference to a modern compilation shows me that this hypercritical gentleman started upon his career as a student of medicine in Dublin, that he subsequently took a German degree, and that after practising for a short time he forsook his profession for novel-writing as being at once more profitable and less laborious. Apart, then, from his talent for producing fiction—of which I would speak with all possible respect— Mr. Lever is an Irish gentleman of the precise class to which the English clergymen, physicians, bankers, civil engineers and merchants, who honoured me by accepting my escort to Italy last year, indisputably belong. By what right, then, does he constitute himself their censor? By what right does he assume them incapable of properly enjoying and intelligently appreciating the wonders of nature, and the treasures of art, brought before them by travel? Drawn from the same sphere of society as himself, educated in a like way, and possessing doubtless many tastes and sympathies in common with him, the only social advantage he can claim is the doubtful one of having lived nearly all his life abroad. It is surely a moot point whether the surroundings and moral tone of the curious little colonies of English people scattered up and down the Continent are so vastly superior to those enforced by public opinion at home, as to entitle the self-expatriated Briton to look down upon us with contempt.'

In Britain the Press tended to take Cook's side. There was no secret about the identity of O'Dowd, whose duty, as Cook's protagonists were quick to point out, was to help tourists abroad, and even their 'bear-leader' if required. With good reason, Cook wrote to the Earl of Clarendon, then Foreign Secretary, pointing out that his business was suffering from Lever's calumnies and asking whether it was fit for a member of the Consular Service to arouse antagonism towards his fellow countrymen in foreign lands. The Foreign Secretary appears to have been able to do little more than express his sympathy, intimating that Lever was covered by his pseudonym, and that there was nothing in what he had written to give official colour to his comments. Lever died in 1872, at his post in the Trieste he had described as 'detestable and damnable,' and the controversy seems to have predeceased him.

The episode did not deter Archibald Campbell Tait, the ailing Archbishop of Canterbury, from placing himself in the hands of Thomas Cook when ordered to spend the winter of 1870-1 on the Riviera. Apart from the eminence of this new client, the occasion was an onerous one for Cook. The Franco-Prussian war, then raging, prevented direct access to the south. It was therefore necessary to conduct the archiepiscopal party through Belgium, Germany and Austria, over the Brenner Pass to Genoa and thence to the Riviera. It may serve to temper the sharp tongue of the Consul at Trieste and others, as well as to provide a personal glimpse of Thomas Cook himself, to quote the account of this journey given many years later by one of the party, Charlotte Lady Wake, in her reminiscences: 'The Franco-German war was in progress, and to make the journey at all showed considerable enterprise. It was necessary to cross by Ostend and to travel through Germany. In the light of modern conditions and habits, it is startling to realize that the party numbered in all sixteen. There was the Archbishop and Mrs. Tait and the three girls; there was his sister, Lady Wake, and her daughter; there was a chaplain and a doctor, and servants. The journey was personally supervised and accompanied by Mr. Thomas Cook himself. Lady Wake has recorded: "It would be the height of injustice not to acknowledge our obligations to Mr. Cook, who, on hearing of our projected journey, volunteered himself to act as the Archbishop's courier. The effects were marvellous. From the first start we always found most comfortable saloon carriages ready for us. As we neared each halting-place for the night, the landlord of our hotel met us at the station in advance; and when we arrived, three carriages, beautifully appointed, were in readiness to convey our party, sixteen in number, to the hotel, where we found not only our rooms prepared for us, but the names of each of our party over the doors, including those of the ladies' maids. Cook knew by instinct exactly what would suit each of us. Naturally I felt great curiosity to see for myself the magician who wrought these wonders, for at the crowded stations I had not been able to distinguish him. My surprise was great when a quiet, middle-aged man, very much like a home-staying, retired tradesman was pointed out to me, walking up and down the platform, with his hands in his pockets, seemingly taking notice of no one. He could not speak a word of any language but his own..."

A glance at *Punch* of the 'seventies and 'eighties shows that one of the most persistent sources of humour was the activities of Anglo-Saxon tourists on the Continent, their struggles with foreign tongues, their lack of poise, their social misfortunes and, of course, their encounters with foreigners, themselves a never-failing source of humour. Cook and his excursionists were picked on a good deal, particularly in the drawings of Du Maurier towards the end of the 'seventies. These minor assaults provided Cook with a sturdy protagonist in the person of the great George Augustus Sala. A counter G. A. S. attack on Du Maurier appeared in the *Illustrated London News* in 1880: 'Is it not time that the stupid and unjust practice of sneering at Cook's Tourists came to an end? Here is bright, clever Mr. Du Maurier, indulging, in the pages of *Punch*, in a gratuitous and very cruel fling at the "personally conducted" patrons of Messrs. Thomas Cook & Son. The scene of Mr. Du Maurier's drawing is laid in the garden of a hotel somewhere in Italy; and a very snobbish-looking English youth, who has left his crutch and toothpick at home, but has brought his wide-awake hat

POMP AND CIRCUMSTANCE. THE KAISER VISITS THE HOLY LAND

THEIR COOK-ORGANIZED ENCAMPMENT

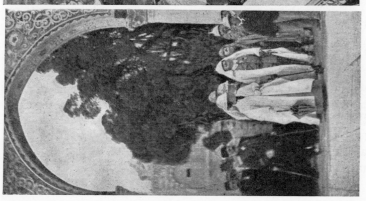

THE KAISER AND KAISERINA

with him, observes to the waiter, "You have rather a large party this afternoon, Sandro"; to which the attendant replies with a grin, "Yes, Sare, it is von of Mistare Cook's parties. Dere are twenty-tree patients in all." The patients are represented by a crowd of deplorable men, women, and children, some of whom look like incurable valetudinarians, and others like congenital idiots. In the first place, Mr. Du Maurier, who, inferentially, belongs to the Latin race, ought to be aware that the word "patient" in France and Italy is not usually applied to a sick person. He is in French "*le malade*," and in Italian "*un ammalato*" or "*un sofferonti*." Only Mrs. Gen'l Gilflory (who has lived so long abroad) would talk about "ung Doctor ay say pashiongs"—or patients.

'In the next place I may say that I have met with many hundreds of Cook's Tourists in the course of my travels; and I never could discern any difference between them and other English travellers on the Continent, save that they were, as a rule, better behaved and more anxious to acquire information than are the general run of "T.G's" (travelling gents; the abbreviation dates from the days of the Crimean War) of the "stuck-up" order. I have been told that one of the most illustrious of English statesmen has been heard to say that he regards Mr. Thomas Cook and Mr. John Hullah as two of the most important social benefactors that this age has seen.'

It seems almost certain that Cook got some publicity in the lectures and entertainments given by 'Arthur Sketchley' whose popularity in this wise was enhanced by the humorous adventures of his once-famous and ubiquitous 'Mrs. Brown' in the series of little yellow-backed books with illustrated covers to be seen on every railway bookstall in the 'sixties and 'seventies. Everywhere that the travelled Sketchley went, Mrs. Brown was sure to go, and Cook probably had a not disinterested hand in the arrangements. In 1864, we find him making editorial mention in *The Excursionist* of Sketchley's lectures on

'Trips to Paris,' and Sketchley wrote a straightforward account of Cook's activities in *Out for a Holiday with Cook's Excursion through Switzerland and Italy*, a small book which, to compensate for a lack of date on the title-page, carries a dedication to T. Cook.

It is more than likely that Thomas Cook's nonconformist scruples kept him away from the theatre. Nevertheless, just after his death, it was considered to be a piece of practical good business when it was proposed to plug his name in a production at the Gaiety Theatre. The correspondence revealing the financial background to the perpetuation of Cook in song has fortunately been preserved. The show was *A Runaway Girl*, a musical play by Seymour Hicks and Harry Nicholls, with lyrics by Aubrey Hopwood and Harry Greenbank, set to the tuneful music of Lionel Monckton and Ivan Caryll. Verbal negotiations began in January, 1898, and the next month a letter went from Seymour Hicks to the firm: 'I cannot send you the second act . . . I may, however, tell you that the advertisement for Mr. Cook is just as good as in the first Act . . . I shall be very glad indeed if you will kindly let me have an answer from Mr. Cook as to whether he will agree to the sum of £200 for the advertisement . . . as if he does not wish to entertain the matter, Mr. Edwardes will substitute the name of Smith or any other imaginary firm.' This was followed a few days afterwards by a letter addressed personally to one of the Cooks: 'I will let you have the second Act as soon as I can . . . I have worked Cook's coupons into the Finale of the first Act musically, and into the dialogue.' Some weeks later Seymour Hicks wrote again: 'There is a musical number entitled "Follow the Man from Cook's"; a Cook's Agent in the Piece; the low comedy part is a Cook's courier, and many of the characters are Cook's Tourists; there is also an Octet in it.'

The terms of the agreement were drafted on the following lines: 'Your firm and its system of business being

mentioned in a favourable and satisfactory manner in the
plot of a Play entitled, provisionally: "The English Girl"
—such Play to be produced by the Gaiety Company in
Great Britain & Ireland, Australia & the United States,
the sum of £200 . . . first instalment £100 on production
. . . second & final . . . immediately after the one
hundredth representation . . .'

A concerted piece at the end of the first Act consisted of
three verses and a refrain which ran:

> 'Oh, follow the man from Cook's,
> The wonderful man from Cook's;
> And whether your stay be short or long,
> He'll show you the sights.
> He can't go wrong:
> Oh, follow the man from Cook's,
> The wonderful man from Cook's.
> It's twenty to one
> You've plenty of fun,
> So follow the man from Cook's!'

Needless to say a *Punch* parodist seized his opportunity:

> 'Oh, bother the man from Cook's!
> The worrying man from Cook's!
> For whether he's booked by week or day,
> He'll tire you to death and call it play,
> Oh, bother the man from Cook's!
> The worrying man from Cook's!
> It's twenty to one you say when he's done:
> Oh, murder the man from Cook's!'

It seems only compensatory to round this chapter off
with what Gladstone—then between his third and fourth
term of office as Prime Minister, an already established
client of the Cook office, had to say about Cook's activities.
In reviewing the second part of Tennyson's *Locksley Hall*,

he referred to the triumph of cheap communication in which England had led the world, and added: 'Among the humanizing contrivances of the age, I think notice is due to the system founded by Mr. Cook, and now largely in use, under which numbers of persons, and indeed whole classes, have for the first time found easy access to foreign countries, and have acquired some of that familiarity with them, which breeds not contempt but kindness.'

CHAPTER EIGHTEEN

Wars

———————————

THE popular discovery of freedom of movement was the Cooks' greatest ally. Human violence, war and rumours of war, curtailing or prohibiting travel have usually been the enemies most to be dreaded. A travel agency, implying liberty of choice and circulation, is the very antithesis of war. Though the Cook concern, founded and consolidated during the golden years of Victorian peace, has survived a century of conflicts, it has done so only by flexibility and improvization, serving the unexpected demands made upon it in emergency.

In the early years, Thomas Cook's closest approach to violence was made when he was conducting a party through Greece in the spring of 1870. In Athens, on the advice of the British Minister, he made a request to the Greek Government for a military escort to accompany his party as far as Marathon. His request was refused and he was forced to cancel this part of the trip. A private party, including Lord and Lady Muncaster, however, was more successful, and duly set out for Marathon with what proved to be a wholly inadequate escort. The famous brigand band led by the brothers Arvanitaki, believing that they were ambushing a Cook tour, attacked and overpowered the party. Two days later, Lord Muncaster arrived in Athens, having been set at liberty on condition that he raised a ransom of £32,000, free pardons for the gang and the release of certain of its members then in gaol. When the Greek Government refused this demand and sent a strong military force against the brigands, four of the hapless tourists were at once executed—a tragic reminder to Cook that the Europe he was so busy opening up in the interests of peaceful travel still contained many perils for the unwary.

The Franco-Prussian war of 1870-1, already recalled in the reminiscences of Lady Wake, afforded the first great test of Cook's resourcefulness in a war emergency. Its outbreak found Cook tourists stranded in many parts of Europe. Its declaration, in fact, came so suddenly that it caught both father and son away from base, each with parties of British and American tourists visiting the Passion Play at Oberammergau. As neutrals, the tourists were in no danger, though many of them found the German railways closed to civilian traffic, and others could not make full use of the tickets they had bought, yet most made a rush return to the British Isles, travelling as best they could. With typical meticulousness, Cook refunded money to all who had been disappointed, without waiting to be asked. Then father and son worked out roundabout routes for travellers to the Riviera or Italy, and for those who wished to travel on to the East from Brindisi. By thus bringing order into wartime confusion in Europe they gained many customers who might not in peacetime have considered using their services. It was now that they initiated and popularized a new form of international ticket which gave passengers a choice of route. The younger Cook made a deal with the German railways for facilitating Far and Near Eastern traffic by way of the Brenner Pass to Brindisi, arrangements which enabled him as soon as the war was over to force the hands of the French railways who hitherto had opposed his organization of through traffic. Though Fraser Rae, writing in the distant 'nineties, could describe that war as being 'the most severe in living memory,' it was in fact so localized that by energetic neutrality, the Cooks suffered little in the progressive expansion of their business. When the war ended it might, indeed, almost have been said that they, with a characteristic mingling of philanthropy and good business, 'cashed in' on the issue.

At the time of the Armistice, a Mansion House Committee raised funds and bought provisions for the relief of those who had been besieged in Paris. The Committee appointed Colonel Stuart Wortley and Mr. George Moore as their emissaries, and it was arranged, probably at his own suggestion, that John Mason Cook should accompany them to give what assistance he could in getting the provisions through.

A description of this trip written by the younger Cook on twenty sheets of blue, business-headed notepaper is still in the possession of Mrs. F. H. Cook, his daughter-in-law. Clearly it was his intention to follow his father's example in keeping the Press informed of his activities: 'Being most anxious to see of what service I could be to personal friends in Paris and also desirous of ascertaining from Railway administrations how long it will be before something like a direct service for the conveyance of passengers to Paris will be established, I decided to start, which decision was promptly acted upon.

'I left London Bridge at 8.15 p.m. on Tuesday, Jany. 31st with a special train conveying the Mails and crossed from Newhaven to Dieppe with about 100 passengers, arriving there about 5.0 a.m. Wednesday, Feby. 1st . . .

'Colonel Stuart Wortley and Mr. George Moore crossed by the same steamer in charge of 75 tons of provisions from the City of London for the City of Paris, and at the request of the General Manager of the Newhaven & Dieppe route I had promised to assist them all I could in getting their provisions conveyed from Dieppe as speedily as possible.'

From Dieppe, there being no passenger service on the railways, Cook posted to Rouen where he interviewed an official at the Prussian-occupied Prefecture, who promised him help through the headquarters of the Duke of Wurtemburg at Amiens. Thence he rode to Nantes, but found no horse available for him to post on. He therefore made his way, night-walking by moonlight under the guidance of a *franc-tireur*, to Mezières. There he found a horse that carried him to the outskirts of Paris where he had great difficulty in obtaining a permit to enter the city.

'On Saturday morning Feby. 4th I obtained admission but had to fight my way through the densest mass of human beings I have ever encountered, before I could cross the bridge. I walked into Paris by the Avenue of the Grand Army. . . . Whilst walking down the Champs Élysées the first thing I saw was a load of grain in Midland Ry. Co's sacks being put into a large mansion which had been converted into a warehouse.'

Within the City he evidently found conditions not so bad as they had been painted, and he at once took the opportunity of looking up M. Chardon, the hotel proprietor who had co-operated in the Exhibition hotel venture in the Boulevard Haussmann, to find out what would be the likelihood of accommodation and entertainment for British tourists desiring (a little ghoulishly, perhaps, by modern standards) to see defeated Paris during the Armistice.

'During the two days I spent in Paris, I lived pretty much as the besieged residents, and I must say the fare was not unpalatable to me after my arduous journey. My friends told me the bread was at its worst, but I did not consider it much worse than the coarse oat-cake of the Scotch highlands; the horse-flesh soup was excellent; the horse-flesh not at all to be despised, but then it was not being forced down me at the point of the bayonet and it was a novelty, which I have no doubt would soon have worn off.

'. . . My return journey from Paris was made in 30 hours, particulars of which I have given in the London daily papers.

'. . . On my return I brought the first report from Col. Wortley and Mr. Geo. Moore, announcing to the Lord Mayor the commencement of the distribution of the food and I have to-night sent off a special messenger with dispatches from the Mansion House meeting of to-day. I have no doubt by this time there are plenty of provisions in Paris for those who have the means to buy them and my advice to all the relief committees is to send money . . .'

Before that descriptive ink of his could have been properly dry, he had organized his Paris excursionists. A party, one hundred and fifty strong, left a few days after his return. This piece of enterprise by the younger Cook evidently impressed Westminster as well as the City. James White, Member for Brighton, a few weeks later, condemning the cost of moving the troops over the British railway system, declared that if Thomas Cook & Son were given the job 'the country would probably be a gainer to the extent of something like £120,000 or £130,000, while the soldiers would find the change attended by a great increase of comfort.'

During the Commune period, Paris was cut off once more from the outside world, and the French railways were closed to passenger traffic until the Peace Treaty with Germany was signed in June. The younger Cook, alert as ever, re-entered Paris on the heels of the French troops who marched from Versailles. British and American tourists, he knew, were clamouring for Paris. He was ready to cope with a roaring trade.

Good fortune such as this did not as a rule follow war, though a successful Cook participation in the Sudan campaign in the 'eighties will be mentioned later. The American war in Cuba in the 'nineties caused a temporary recession in the considerable volume of American business which by that time had grown up.

The Boer war had an adverse effect on European travel owing to the unpopularity of the British on the Continent. In South Africa, Cooks' opened offices in order, according to a former member of the staff still living, 'to help the troops in every way they could.' It seems that the more conventional side of the business concerned shipping; but the British Government also commissioned the firm to superintend the deportation of 'foreign undesirables.' This task entailed the provision of each deportee with the cheapest possible ticket to his home destination, together with a sovereign in cash, and seeing him off on his journey out of the country. It was not one to stimulate future customers. Indeed, it took the firm some time to live down the memory of this unenviable duty.

Compared with the global campaigns of our own times, the beginning at least of the First World War seemed curiously localized. Cooks managed to run winter sports excursions to Switzerland, Norway and Canada in 1915, and were still catering for holiday-makers in the South of France, Spain, Italy, Switzerland and North Africa. The following year there was pleasure travel in the French Riviera, Spain, Madeira, North Africa, Egypt and further afield. But in 1914, at the outbreak of war, there were upwards of six thousand tourists (not all of them Cooks') stranded on the Continent, most of them in Switzerland. Edward Huskisson, a Cook man since 1898 and later General Manager of the firm, was sent to rescue them. He took £500 in gold on his person, set out at the same time as a King's Messenger, and arrived in Switzerland, as he proudly recalls, two days before him. There were no travel priorities in that war. It was a matter of pushing and knowing the right people. Nor, oddly enough, were there the frontier examinations or passports—the only two countries requiring them being Turkey and Russia. Huskisson spent three months in Geneva despatching elaborately-routed special trains carrying eight hundred people at a time and financing them. He even managed to rescue British tourists from enemy territory. Two large parties who had been trapped by the war at Carlsbad, where they were taking the cure, came through by special train

to Geneva, whence they were despatched to the Channel
ports with even their luggage intact. This relief work
was officially and gratefully acknowledged by Parliament.

The staff at the time already numbered several thousand
and many of the men volunteered in groups, leaving on the
same day for the same regiment, their jobs being guaranteed by the third generation of Cooks who were then in
control of the concern. The Netherlands being neutral, the
Cook office in Amsterdam naturally became a clearing-
house for Enemy Mail, the handling of which was taken
over entirely by the firm. Meanwhile most of the offices
remained open. There was a steady demand for tours within
Britain, particularly in London, even during the most
tragic period of the conflict. This, together with a special
service for the armed forces including forwarding of mail
and collection of pay warrants, kept the structure of the
organization together. Nor were the possibilities of new
overseas business overlooked. Edward Huskisson was sent
to Russia to work out an agreement with the Russian
railways just before the Kerensky regime. He found the
doomed Imperialists characteristically evasive and dilatory,
and returned only just in the nick of time. As soon as the war
was over, there was the melancholy task of dealing with the
traffic of mourners and sightseers to the former battlefields
—a far more elaborate enterprise, alas, than the post-war
efforts of John Mason Cook nearly fifty years before.

The effects of the beginning of a Second World War
were, of course, drastic and immediate. Private travel
overseas ceased almost as soon as the Cook organization
had brought back the last peacetime pleasure-seekers, and
had despatched neutral visitors to their homes. Though
with a skeleton staff and many of their offices closed, the
firm took on a number of special commitments. The first
of these was the evacuation of thousands of children to
parents overseas, particularly in the Far East. This work,
which was independent of the Government-sponsored
Overseas Reception Board, entailed meeting children, of

ages ranging from three to seventeen, when they arrived in London from their schools and taking full responsibility for them until they sailed. It continued through the anxious months of 1940 until September, when the sinking of the *City of Benares* by a U-boat—and perhaps the spirit of that note which went from Winston Churchill to the Home Secretary: '. . . I entirely deprecate any stampede from this country'—brought such evacuation activities to a close.

Once again Cooks opened an Enemy Mail Department. As before, this was the sole agency for the exchange of letters between people in Britain and in the enemy-occupied countries. Complementary to it was a department known as Continental Communications which carried out enquiries about the welfare of friends and relatives on the other side—a service unhappily not extended to penetrate the Iron Curtain of our own times. The Expeditionary Forces Supply Service was Cook-run. Seven hundred thousand parcels were packed and dispatched to every theatre of war—and ninety-five per cent got there. Staff who were not in uniform were also associated with the Red Cross scheme for Prisoner of War parcels.

Being expert in Movement Control—that military magic by which many of us have been shoved around in uniform—a group of the present Cook staff have kept themselves in readiness for any future emergency. In 1951 they formed an army unit consisting of forty-two officers and two hundred and fifty-three other ranks, which assembled for annual training at the Royal Engineers Transportation Centre in Hampshire.

To complete this war story, it should be mentioned that the Cook resources in the Near East were not without significance in World War II. But for an explanation of the very existence of these resources we must return again to those days when wars were still followed by peace and when the Cooks stood impatiently upon the threshold of that latter nineteenth-century world that was powered by steam.

CHAPTER NINETEEN

The Holy Land *De Luxe*

E VEN in the 'forties when his scope was limited to the British Isles, Thomas Cook had hankered to visit the lands of the Bible. If his inspiration was spiritual, his practical enthusiasm owed much to his first contact as a temperance advocate with James Silk Buckingham, who was an experienced traveller in the Middle East. But Cook had to wait to realize his dream of travel in the Holy Land even longer than his much-delayed discovery of the New World. It was not until he and his son had consolidated their Continental enterprises in 1868 that he set out for Constantinople, Beyrout, Jaffa, Alexandria and Cairo. Something of the spirit in which this journey was made is reflected in Fraser Rae's account of it. 'The Crusaders went thither to slay the Saracens: Mr. Thomas Cook went to devise plans for rendering the Holy Land generally accessible to his countrymen. There was nothing belligerent in his piety or sanguinary in his nature. His pride was to conduct his countrymen in the pleasant and picturesque paths of peace.'

In this long-cherished enterprise, Cook was not by any means a pioneer. Since the times of the Crusaders the Holy Land had been a place of pilgrimage with a long history of organized travel. It was travel, moreover, which even in the third quarter of the nineteenth century could only be undertaken safely on a grand scale, a venture for the wealthy or influential who would assemble about them a lavish cavalcade with armed protection and who would be ready at all times to pay handsomely for safe conduct. 'Before Mr. Thomas Cook led his first party through Palestine,' wrote Fraser Rae, 'travellers were at the mercy of savage chiefs, who made them pay dearly for the protection which they afforded, or the permission which they granted to pass through their districts. These chiefs were as fickle as they were avaricious, and as dilatory as they were exacting. Now, the plans of travel laid in London are carried out to the letter and the day, in the Eastern regions which Cook's tourists traverse. Moreover, the element of danger has been almost entirely eliminated, and those who would have hesitated to trust themselves in Palestine as it was a generation ago, now go thither without fear, and their confidence in the measures taken by the Messrs. Cook is fully justified.'

The confidence of the redoubtable Thomas seems to have been equal to the intricacies of Middle Eastern negotiation. Immediately on his return from his exploratory trip, in December, 1868, he advertised a tour to Palestine and the Nile for the following spring. Thirty-two 'ladies and gentlemen' took tickets to the Nile and Palestine, and thirty to Palestine only. For their accommodation, two camps were established in Palestine. On the Nile, arrangements were made to hire two steamers, a transaction which was the beginning of an association of Cook's name with Egypt in general and the Nile in particular. This—of inestimable importance both to the development of the Cook business and of the vogue for Egypt as a tourist centre—will be mentioned in a separate chapter. Though Cook had founded his fortune upon steam travel, with occasional recurrence to horses, he seems to have been undaunted either by the cumbersome mechanics or by the dangers of travel through Palestine.

A couple of decades after his first visit, safe-conduct

often depended upon primitive transactions between the Government, local sheikhs and those who made the journey. Of travel in the eighteen-eighties, Mrs. Vester* has written, '. . . the country was unsafe and the Turkish Government conceived a clever device to guard travellers. One of the villages was considered the "robbers' home" of Eastern Palestine. The family of the paramount sheikh was officially made responsible for the safety of the Jericho Road. All travellers paid a fee to this family, and a member would then accompany the party. This made the village with the sheikh and his family responsible for safety and insured no molestation. Woe betide the party that had not paid its fee . . .'

Even after the wiles of railway managers, negotiations with such characters as Sheikh Mustifa (who personally accompanied more important travellers riding a beautiful Arab mare decorated with rich oriental trappings) must have taxed the Christian patience of Thomas Cook. He left no record, however, of exasperation; though he was eloquent enough about this new field where business opportunity and religious enlightenment so delightfully combined to stimulate him. With his usual thoroughness he faced up to the dangers; but there is no doubt that his potential customers were nervous. 'Will any lady traveller who has done the journey through Palestine tell me if it can be easily and comfortably accomplished by ladies?' wrote a correspondent during the 'seventies in *All the World Over*, a monthly travel magazine published by the Cooks at Ludgate Circus. 'My wife and daughter are both extremely anxious to accompany me, and I should be really thankful for a plain, unvarnished statement of the facts. I should say that they have travelled all over Switzerland, and have tolerably strong nerves.'

The reply to this correspondent was ostensibly signed by a satisfied customer but seems to have been inspired, to say the least, from Ludgate Circus: 'Two or three years

* *Our Jerusalem*, by Bertha Spafford Vester (Evans, 1951).

ago I made one of a party in which there were seven other
ladies. Only two of us were used to horseback, although
we had had some little experience in travelling. We started
our pilgrimage in the Holy Land at Jaffa; our horses were
good, and we were able to obtain English saddles. Our first
night was spent in the Valley of Ajalon, and here we had
our first experience of tent life. A Turkey carpet covered
the floor; a comfortable iron bedstead was ready for each
of us (three ladies in one tent), with good clean sheets
and blankets, and everything in all respects necessary for
comfort. Each day we had as good a breakfast in our large
dining-saloon as we should have had at a first-class hotel;
every day we had a substantial picnic lunch; and in the
evening, after the toils of the day, our table d'hôte of
soups, fish, flesh and fowl, and all the luxuries of life,
was more enjoyable than I have ever known table d'hôte
elsewhere. For thirty days this lasted, almost every day
pitching our tents at some fresh place, except when at
Jerusalem. Although we experienced two or three days'
wet and a famous Syrian storm, although we slept in the
dews of Hermon, and bathed, when heated, in the cold
waters of Jordan, none of us were unwell, nor had such an
uneasy sneeze prophetic of a cold. My advice to C. V. S.
is to take his wife and daughter unhesitatingly. I should
mention that we were in one of Cook's parties, and I do
not know how we should have fared had this not been so,
as we never had to drive one single bargain for anything
all the time we were in Egypt and Palestine, and all
arrangements were first-class in every respect.'

To achieve such a satisfactory sense of well-being in the
Victorian traveller the standard equipment was formidable.
For a party of sixty pilgrims to the Holy Land, twenty-
one sleeping tents were needed, together with two tents
described as dining-saloons, and three cooking tents. These
had to be pitched and struck at every halt. Sixty-five
saddle-horses, eighty-seven pack-horses, an unspecified
number of mules and twenty-eight asses carried people and

THE GORDON RELIEF EXPEDITION (1884)

OVER A NILE CATARACT

Illustrated London News

THE 'ILLUSTRATED LONDON NEWS' ARTIST'S IMPRESSION OF THE JOURNEY TO KHARTOUM

baggage. Fifty-six muleteers, three dragomans, eighteen camp servants and five watchdogs were required to serve the party.

Something of the spirit with which Thomas Cook approached the realization of his vision of the Holy Land is expressed in one of his characteristic letters to the press at home. His heart still in the Midlands, he wrote a letter from Beyrout to the *Stamford Mercury* some four years after his first exploratory visit. For its mingling of piety, common sense, good business and good intentions, it deserves, I think, quotation at some length. 'Out of a complete list of 50 travellers under our arrangements, 45 have come forward to Palestine, a very few making a short tour to Jerusalem, &c. and 40 coming through the land from Jaffa to Solomon's Pools, Hebron, Bethlehem, Mount Tabor, the Dead Sea, Jordan, Jericho, Bethany, over the Mount of Olives to Jerusalem. It is from the summit of the Mount of Olives that Jerusalem, once "the joy of the whole earth" is best seen, and my plan was to let as little of it, on the west side, be seen as possible, until the glorious sight of walls, domes, minarets, flat and dome roofed houses, burst at one view on the astonished beholder; and a glorious view we had on the bright day that we encamped under the walls of the city. Here we spent, on Mount Zion, a lovely sabbath, the worship of the Anglo-Prussian church being most highly appreciated. Prayers were read morning and evening by the famous traveller and Eastern explorer, just escaped from a brigand sheik in the land of Moab, Dr. Tristam . . .

'Our cavalcade of 40 saddle horses, 60 baggage mules, and 22 donkeys with nearly 50 dragomans, servants and muleteers, left Jerusalem for Samaria, Galilee and the Lebanon . . . to the Beyrout.

'The pleasantest life in Palestine travel is in tents, furnished with iron bedsteads, wool beds, carpeted floors, and an ample supply of excellent, well-cooked food. "Tim Tom" is generally sounded to wake us up at 6 a.m.

(sometimes sooner); in half an hour the tents are struck; in an hour we get breakfast, and by 8 o'clock all is ready for departure. After from four to five hours riding we rest for a couple of hours, under olive trees or in some cool shade, where fresh water can be obtained, and where we take lunch. While thus resting the mules get in advance, and when we arrive at our appointed camping ground we find our movable hotel ready, and resume occupation of the same sleeping apartment, the same bed and bedding, with the same numbered napkin, that we left in the morning. Our sensible and enduring little horses, having been trained to the work of the country, climb up and descend along hill sides with remarkable discretion and safety, something like a cat picking his way among chimney pots. The mules are wonders of endurance and strength, carrying all sorts of heavy loads, and never stopping from morning till night. Your farmer readers will be interested to know that a horse of fair average character is worth about 20 *L.* to 25 *L.*, whilst the best of the mules sell for 50 *L.* to 60 *L.*

'Two years ago I saw this land as a land of drought and vegetative desolation, with clouds of locusts filling the air or covering the last green leaves of trees, or withering blades of corn. Now all is fresh and verdant, the hills are covered with beautiful and fragrant herbs and flowers, the valleys and the plains are carpeted with fine crops of wheat and barley, fringed with flowers of the most beautiful hues and varieties. The historical plains of Sharon, where, as Hepworth Dixon says, "bloomed all the roses of imagination," are yielding to the plough, and thousands of acres are covered with grain. Sentimentalism succumbs to utilitarianism, and the land again bids fair to flow with milk and honey, where cultivation is properly attended to. The orange groves of Jaffa are redundant with fine, rich fruit, and the old port is blockaded with cargoes for exportation. I have not previously seen Palestine wearing such a pleasant aspect as it wears to-day . . .'

'May I conclude this letter with a little appeal to your philanthropic readers? Three years ago, when our camps were pitched under the walls of Jerusalem, after a night of violent storms and restlessness, about 70 travellers, camp servants, and muleteers all "slumbered and slept." Past midnight a cry arose that we were robbed. Four or five tents had been entered, and bags, portmanteaux, and trunks, had been taken a short distance, cut open, and plundered of all hard cash and gold articles to the total amount of 650 *L.*, of which £450 *L.* (in French and English gold) was from my own portmanteau. The two thieves were after a short time captured, and from the first of them taken were all the articles recovered and 60 Napoleons in money. On the capture of the second thief, sheep, oxen, land, and a house (at Bethlehem) were placed at my disposal. All except the house were sold, and I got back nearly 200 *L.* The house was new and strongly built, but not finished internally. Our indefatigable British Consul at Jerusalem holds the writings, and the upset price is 100 *L.* I am anxious to make it over to Bishop Gobat's church, schools and hospital, and am willing to sink 25 *L.* in its price (giving the thief credit for 100 *L.* on account of his debt of restitution, for which he will be liable at any time under Turkish law). If friends of Christian education will send 75 *L.* say in donations of a pound cash—to our office, 98, Fleet-street, London, I will transfer the property to the Jews' Society of London, under which the church and property on Mount Zion, Jerusalem, is held, and the property will then be employed in teaching honesty and truth.'

That the leisurely opulence of this form of travel lingered on well into this century, is recalled by Mrs. Vester, whom I have already quoted: 'Such camps were magnificent, the equipment sumptuous, and the service excellent. They were constantly used by tourists. The tents were and still are made in Egypt. Strong sailcloth is used on the outside and this is lined with indigo blue every inch of which is covered with bright patchwork in arabesque patterns. The camp consisted of a bedroom tent for each person or couple, and every morning a tin bath-tub would be dragged into the tent by the attendant. Hot and cold water stood beside the tub in big containers, usually Standard Oil tins. A large tent with double poles was used for dining- and sitting-room with comfortable camp chairs.

'The kitchen tent contained a stove consisting of an iron frame on legs with places for a charcoal fire. The camp cooks were excellent, and the waiters well trained. In those days of leisurely travel, the camp provided the ideal way, and they were used by Thomas Cook & Son and all tourist contractors. These equipments were commandeered by the Turkish Army in 1914, and that ended camp life on the grand style. When travel started up again after the war good hotels had been built. Automobiles took the place of carriages and horses and changed the tempo of travel.'

During the last three decades of the nineteenth century, the Cooks went into the business on a grand scale. In the 'nineties they had enough camping equipment to accommodate a thousand tourists under canvas at the same time and during peak seasons made use of more than a thousand horses. Not all the pilgrims used the saddle. The Cooks noticed the practical advantages of the specially-built landaus used by travellers in the Alps. They had a number of these carriages built for them in Switzerland and exported them to the Holy Land to carry their tourists. By the end of the century some twelve thousand pilgrims to the Holy Land had passed through their hands. These included the King of Servia, several Russian Dukes —and a future King of England.

In 1882, the Prince of Wales, afterwards King Edward VII, authorized the British Consul in Jerusalem to make arrangements with Cook's to organize the visit of Prince Albert Victor and Prince George to the Holy Land. It fell to a member of the third generation of the family,

Frank Henry Cook, therefore, to accompany the future King George V upon this tour and his efforts earned him a testimonial from Marlborough House signed by that Canon Dalton, the Prince's tutor who, as the Duke of Windsor, was to write in his memoirs, 'could not be held responsible for his son's espousal of the doctrine of public ownership of the means of production.'

> 'Marlborough House, Pall Mall,
> September 20th, 1882.

'Dear Sirs,—All the arrangements made for the convenience of the two Princes and their companions during their forty days' stay in the Holy Land gave their Royal Highnesses and every member of the party the utmost satisfaction. Mr. F. H. Cook, whose company we enjoyed the greater part of the time, and your agent or representative at Jerusalem, were both most indefatigable in doing everything they possibly could to conduce to the success of the expedition. We went over nearly six hundred miles, and some of the day's marches were longer than so large a party usually accomplishes. But what was designed was always carried out, spite of weather and other drawbacks, and we owe you every thanks for the energy and promptitude with which each difficulty as it arose was always faced and overcome.

> Believe me, dear Sirs,
> Yours very faithfully,
> (Signed)   John N. Dalton.'

Not the least impressive aspect of the affair was that Frank Cook, who had been educated at a British public school and in Germany, was at that time in his twentieth year, not much older than his princeling charges.

Experience of royal personages and knowledge of the German language fitted him to play a leading part in one of the most spectacular and vainglorious progresses suffered by the Holy Land in modern history. In 1898, the year *The Man From Cook's* became a popular hit at the Gaiety,

Frank Cook was sent to Hamburg for consultations with the Hofmeister of the German Emperor. Kaiser Wilhelm II had had his visions about the Holy Land. Contemporary cynics believed that these were closely related to an obsession with the *Drang nach Osten*. Certainly His Imperial Majesty had been ostentatious in his courtship of his future World War I allies, the Turks; and his proposal to visit the lands of the Bible was to be a momentous affair for their Turkish ruler, the Sultan Abdul-Hamid. Whatever might be the underlying political motives, the peg upon which hung the proposed German royal visit to Palestine was a religious one. Twenty years before, Kaiser Wilhelm I had been presented by the Sultan of Turkey with a property which had formerly been the Palestine headquarters of the Order of St. John of Jerusalem wherein the Knights Hospitalers had maintained their hospice for pilgrims and their infirmary for the sick. This had been converted and rebuilt as the Lutheran Church of the Redeemer, and the Kaiser was to attend its consecration, planned for October 31st, the anniversary of the day on which Martin Luther nailed his thesis to the church door in Wittenberg.

The Imperial tour was said to be inspired and organized by Dr. Barkhausen of Berlin, the President of the Evangelical Church Council for the Jerusalem Expedition.

In the British religious press, political motives were denied. *The Quiver*, which printed a nine-page illustrated article as a trailer to the tour, wrote: 'The undertaking is a pious and domestic, and *not* a political one, spite of several assertions to the contrary; and all who have the cause of true religion at heart cannot but rejoice that there will be another pulpit from which the risen Saviour will be proclaimed to the residents of God's chosen land.'

For a pious and domestic undertaking, the imperial progress did not lack grandeur. The royal party travelled by train from Berlin to Trieste where they embarked on the *Midnight Sun*, an English vessel flying the English flag.

Thence they steamed by way of Venice and Egypt to
Constantinople for a meeting with Abdul-Hamid, who
had fitted his Yildiz Palace with thousands of new-fangled
gas jets for their greater illumination. Their reception in
Palestine was no less prodigal, for the Turks had built a
new jetty at Haifa specially for their landing. Here it was
that the Cooks took over control, enabling *Punch* to refer
to the imperial pilgrims as 'Cook's Crusaders.'

What was described as a modest military element
'consisting only of about sixteen men, eight of them
belonging to the Imperial Body Gendarmerie, and eight
to the Kaiserin's bodyguard' had arrived 'some little time
beforehand to accustom themselves to the habits of the
country.' No doubt they displayed in advance the decoration specially designed for the occasion and known as the
'Jerusalem Cross' which was to be worn by all who had
made the journey from Berlin. 'On that tour,' Frank Cook
recalled in after life, 'we had about one hundred and
twenty Germans including the Emperor and Empress and
their suites, about one hundred Turkish pashas and their
suites, sent by the Sultan to do honour to the Emperor,
and about twenty-five journalists, mostly English.' He
added with slight relish: 'I rode into Jerusalem in front of
the State procession when the ex-Kaiser entered the city,
much to the annoyance of the German tourists who were
there and did not like to see an Englishman taking the
lead and having all the arrangements in hand.'

Like other Cook's tourists, the whole party went under
canvas—but with an imperial difference. Sultan Abdul-
Hamid offered tents, horses and vehicles which at first
were declined lest it should be thought that such trappings
might lend a political significance to a religious occasion.
These scruples were happily overcome, and the Sultan
supplemented the Cook equipment with much oriental
splendour—though the Germans themselves shipped a
certain amount of prefabricated asbestos hutments in
case the tentage proved inadequate. 'I was asked,' writes

Mrs. Vester, 'by the Turkish authorities in charge of the arrangements to select from any house belonging to a Turkish subject in Jerusalem furniture and carpets which would be appropriate to furnish the royal tents.'

The Kaiser made most of the journey on horseback, the Kaiserin riding in an open carriage. They visited the Holy Sepulchre—specially renovated for the occasion by the Sultan—on foot. Jerusalem was decorated, beflagged and illuminated for the pilgrims. A part of the city wall was even knocked down to afford an Imperial entry. For a last glimpse of this most splendid fruit of old Thomas Cook's vision of the lands of the Bible, I return to Mrs. Vester's chronicle: 'The carriage road to the Mount of Olives was made for the Kaiser's visit. It passed the American Colony. At the junction of the two roads, that leading to the Mount of Olives going east and the other north-west to Nablus, there was a sharp hairpin bend. On the first trip of the Imperial visitors to the Mount of Olives the whole party stopped at the hairpin bend for some time.

'I remember we were all out looking over the wall of our garden to watch the important visitors pass by, and we were intrigued with their stop. We asked the Cook's representative who accompanied the Imperial company on all their trips what it meant . . .

'(He) . . . told us that the Kaiser had been explaining to his Turkish hosts that the bend was far too sharp and narrow to allow cannon to pass that way. We gave our informant incredulous smiles, but we lived to see German and Austrian howitzers and cannon roll down that widened bend on their way to fight the British.'

The two flags flown respectively over the tents of the Kaiser and Kaiserin are still preserved in the Cook 'museum.'

THOMAS COOK AND A GROUP OF HIS TOURISTS AT POMPEII IN 1868

KING EDWARD VII IS MET BY COOKS REPRESENTATIVE AT THE FOOT OF VESUVIUS

CHAPTER TWENTY

A Conquest of the Nile

IN the year following his exploratory trip to Egypt, Thomas Cook was one of the guests invited by Ferdinand de Lesseps, with whom he was already on friendly terms, on the occasion of the opening of the Suez Canal. I do not know whether he managed to organize a tourist party aboard one of the sixty-eight vessels which followed the Empress Eugenie's inaugural steamer. It was an opportunity he was unlikely to have missed. Certainly he was destined to send more and varied passengers through that canal than most people who attended the ceremony. His friendship with de Lesseps, of which little is now known, links two European names which were to have a lasting influence on travel in Egypt.

Though Thomas Cook initiated the Egyptian tourist traffic, it was his son, John Mason, assisted by the third generation, who developed the great and glorious travel pattern of late Victorian and Edwardian times, something of which has lingered on to the Air Age. After the return, in the spring of 1889, of the thirty-two 'ladies and gentlemen' for whom Thomas had hired his first Nile steamers, the *Benha* and the *Beniscoif*, a demand both from Britain and from America for leisurely, sanitary, and, above all, safe sightseeing trips in Egypt grew prodigiously. Thomas Cook saw the potentialities of the Nile just as he had seen the potentialities of the iron roads of the Midlands more than a quarter of a century before. This time, however, he had by his side his son, grown up to the business of travel, a man of experience and tireless energy, a matured and seasoned caterer for the travelling public. The Cooks knew what their travelling public wanted. Their name would guarantee comfort, safety, cleanliness and punctuality of operation. That guarantee meant value for money. There was plenty of money forthcoming from the leisured classes of Britain and America if the Nile service could be moulded to tourist requirements. Egypt was almost undiscovered as tourist territory. Only by patience and negotiation—neither of them easy in this corrupt and easy-going *milieu*—could Cook promote that discovery.

The first important move came in 1870 when the younger Cook was officially appointed by the Khedive to act as the agent of his Government for passenger traffic on the Nile. In his report to the *Stamford Mercury* two years later, from which quotation has already been made, Thomas Cook was full of enthusiasm: '. . . There is one predominant feeling of interest that underlies all our visits to these lands and waters of biblical history, *i.e.*, the abiding impression that we are travelling amongst and gazing on scenes with which we have been familiarized from our earliest recollections . . .

'Egypt and Palestine constitute the two greatest features in our present programme; but the countries through which we pass to get here, and the places to be visited on our return journey, all contribute to the general interest of a programme covering about 7,000 miles of travel. We have passed through shattered Paris and bleeding France; here inhaled the soft breezes of awakened and united Italy; have sailed over the classic waters of the Adriatic and Mediterranean, amongst the Ionian Islands, and over that wondrous canal in which mingle the waters of the Red Sea and the Mediterranean, which has separated Africa and Asia, and opened a highway and a short way to our great Eastern Dominions; we have made a double trip of 600 miles up and down the Nile, from Cairo to the first cataract . . .

'I said that Egypt and Palestine constitute the two great features of the tour, and a few words on each may not be unacceptable. After briefly scanning Alexandria, which is a sort of Oriental-European conglomerate, with but few attractions, we hastened on to the capital of modern Egypt—Cairo—which presents a strange combination of ancient orientalism with Parisian innovations. . . . But it was on the Nile and by its banks that centred our chief European interest. The section of my party for the Nile tour comprised 31 ladies and gentlemen, and we occupied two of the Khedive's steamers with berths for the exact number. Our tables were abundantly supplied by our co-operative agent for the Nile steamboat traffic, Mr. Eftzeinberger, of the Hotel Victoria, Venice, to whom with myself and son, has been entrusted the entire agency of the service. . . . We spent in all twenty-three days on and adjacent to the Nile, and then, like the Israelites of old, we came from the land "watered with the pools" to this "Land of Promise".'

In 1875, John Mason Cook persuaded the Egyptian Government to pass a passenger steamer over the First Cataract when the Nile was in flood, in order that there should be a regular steamboat service from there to the Second Cataract. He followed this firstly by making a special arrangement for his tourists to use the newly-run mail steamers between Assiout and Assouan and then, most important of all, by obtaining the appointment as sole agent for the postal service on all Government steamers. By 1880, the Egyptian Government were so impressed by the enterprise shown by the Cooks on the Nile that they granted them exclusive control of all passenger steamers in return for which the Cooks undertook to expend large sums in refitting the boats and to conduct the service at their own expense and risk. John Mason

Cook knew what he wanted, and the authorities were finding out what undreamed-of trade his methods could bring. Amid the lassitude and corruption of the Delta of the Khedive, his character stood out. His great physical strength had been developed as a youth in his father's printing works. He had never deviated from his temperance principles, and in this and in many other respects he had shown himself to be a man of great strength of character. On such occasions as his strong arm combined with his forceful personality he must have made a deep impression upon the Egyptians, as this contemporary anecdote may serve to illustrate: '. . . When he first began to open up the Nile—where the difficulties of travel had previously been considered almost insurmountable, the first fleet of boats put upon the river left considerable room for improvement in many respects. They were comparatively crude in their design, and left so much to be desired that Mr. Cook was determined to replace them with better boats. The man who captained the first of the new steamers very much objected to a new kind of steering wheel with which they were fitted, and thought that the first trip would be a good opportunity to prove that what he called "these new-fangled notions" were all wrong.

'Accordingly, directly the party arrived on board, he steered the most erratic course possible, nearly running his ship aground on several occasions. When asked what was the matter he replied that it was impossible to steer a correct course with the new apparatus. Mr. Cook thought otherwise, and, remarking that "a man who can't steer a straight course is no good to me as a captain," it is said, picked up the skipper and dropped him over the side into the Nile, after which he calmly took the wheel himself and kept his course without any trouble.'

The appeal of Egypt to Northern Europeans was as a winter resort, and the benefits of the Nile for invalids were particularly stressed. The improvements of the steamers were followed by better amenities ashore. In 1877, an hotel was opened at Luxor, specially catering for invalids who wished to winter there without moving along the river. The demand proved to be so great that a second hotel was immediately erected, and when even this proved insufficient, one of the steamers was tied up alongside to provide more accommodation. The Cooks were back in the business of beds, but with what a social contrast to the utilitarian accommodation they had provided for the British working-class in London and Paris! Incidentally these hotels marked the beginning of a new policy that the Cooks applied almost exclusively to their Egyptian sphere of activity. Elsewhere in the world, with a few notable exceptions which will be mentioned, they were content to act as agents rather than as proprietors—a decision which it seems to me has always contributed to the flexibility of the concern.

As with the earliest rail excursions in industrial Britain, nothing in Egypt was left to chance. There was a whole range of literature from leaflet and throw-aways to elaborate bound volumes, to tell the hale and the sick alike what to expect and how to enjoy Egypt. Information was offered with a good deal of directness. A note on Money begins with 'By far the most important item in an outfit for Egypt is money, and enough of it, for it must not be forgotten that travelling in the East and Hotel accommodation are expensive.' Some of the prices paid, incidentally, were not by modern standards exorbitant. A twelve weeks' tour with first-class travel and hotels through parts of Egypt, the Nile, Palestine, Syria, Turkey, Greece, the Ionian Islands, Austria, Italy, Switzerland and France, cost 103 guineas in 1868. In 1873, an eighty-five-day tour of Lower Egypt, the Nile and Palestine, cost £120.

I suspect a slight dig at the customers in this piece of advice printed under the heading Daily Life: 'Great caution must be taken against the chilly night air. Very often severe diarrhœa results from carelessness in this respect. Instead of imitating the Arabs in wearing the "fez," it would be much better to imitate them in wearing warm cloth around the loins, etc.'

Perhaps to discourage tourists from dressing-up in the tarboosh, there is no lack of advice about headgear: 'Among the articles of *real* use are helmets, shady or other hats, with puggarees of muslin to protect the head and neck from the sun; also light-coloured umbrellas strong enough to be used as walking-sticks. Some difference of opinion exists as to the best form of head covering. Some think helmets or solar topes indispensable, but this is not accepted universally, and ladies do not greatly favour them, as they are difficult to fit and uncomfortable to wear. Many are satisfied with good wide-awakes or "Terai" hats, and not a few think by far the best of all is a broad-brimmed sailor hat from André's in Bond Street. All ladies should be provided with thin gossamer veils of brown, blue or green, which are an immense comfort and great protection against sand, dust or glare.'

Of such stuff was made the orderly and placid traffic upon the Nile for a decade or more, while three generations of Cooks consolidated their wonderful business and improved the solid comforts afloat. Then, alas, came an interlude of violence and war to cast a deep shadow over the Nile's tourist routine and to rob the paddle-steamers of their guileless and punctual schedules. It began with the revolt by Arabi Pasha against the Khedive who was supported by British armed forces. For several turbulent years a state of revolution and warfare existed which culminated in the bombardment of Alexandria in the summer of 1882. Travel for pleasure came to a standstill, but John Mason Cook was busy meeting the needs of war. After the battle of Tel-el-Kebir, he undertook to transport all the wounded and sick from Cairo to Alexandria by water without making any other charge than the actual cost of running the steamers. For soldiers suffering from enteric fever, he ran special steamer trips up the Nile where eighty to ninety per cent of the patients recovered after some sixteen days—a cure that apparently surprised the doctors. From Pall Mall came another testimonial, this time on behalf of the War Office, by order of the Duke of Cambridge: 'Gentlemen—The Lieutenant-General commanding the troops in Egypt having forwarded for the information of the Field Marshal, the Commander-in-Chief, a report of the cordial assistance rendered by your firm in conveying convalescents for sanitary reasons in your steamers on the Nile, I have now the honour, by desire of his Royal Highness, to convey to you an expression of his thanks for the admirable arrangements made by you on these occasions, by which the troops have greatly benefited. His Royal Highness fully appreciates the public spirit evinced by you in conducting the various services on which you have been employed for military purposes in the above country. (Signed) ARTHUR HERBERT, Lieut.-General, Quartermaster-General.'

Though troop movements in Britain had been held up to ridicule in the House by contrast with the easy ubiquity of Cook excursionists, the War Office seemed to have relied upon the firm for the quick movement of its 'top brass.' Both the Duke of Connaught and his suite and Sir Garnet (afterwards Viscount) Wolseley travelled between London and Cairo on Cook tickets at that time. The latter was despatched for a second tour of duty in the Middle East, and within a few months was to take command of the Nile expedition for the relief of General Gordon at Khartoum, an operation in which the talents of John Mason Cook were to express themselves in no mean fashion.

General Charles Gordon, it will be remembered, had been charged by Gladstone's Government with the evacuation of Europeans from the Sudan and, in the words of the proclamation which he carried with him, 'to restore to the families of the Kings of the Sudan their former independence.' For this tricky, dangerous and controversial mission, he was given a credit of £100,000. At first the

General thought that he could reach Khartoum by going through the Suez Canal, and then overland from Suakin to Berber. The British Government, however, at the instance of Lord Cromer, ordered him to Cairo, where it was arranged that Cook's would be responsible for his conveyance with his staff as far as Korosko on the Nile, whence he would travel by camel to Berber and on to Khartoum. There were complications for Cook in this flattering undertaking. One of the former Sudanese rulers whom the authorities decided to ship back with Gordon, was a certain Emir Abdul Shakour, a member of the Darfour dynasty, described in the journal of Gordon's companion, Colonel Stewart, as 'a common-looking, unintelligent and badly-dressed native.' This unhappy individual, who had been dragged from well-paid exile to act as a political pawn and who had been given two thousand Egyptian pounds, 'a well-embroidered coat and the biggest decoration that could be found,' made frantic efforts to delay General Gordon, who was in a great hurry to start on this, his last, mission. 'Some delay was caused at starting,' wrote Colonel Stewart, 'by the numerous retinue of the Darfour Sultan. Extra carriages had to be put on for the accommodation of his twenty-three wives and a quantity of baggage. At the last moment, his gala uniform was almost forgotten, and there was some commotion until it was found.'

With this commotion settled by the conscientious and tactful Cook, the ill-fated expedition, burdened by the twenty-three royal wives, left Cairo on the night of January 26th, 1884. There is no record of the progress of the expedition to Korosko, where Stewart, amid a spate of letters and telegrams, wrote back to Cairo a little petulantly: 'I shall be very glad when we are actually at Khartoum and face to face with the situation . . .'

Before Gordon mounted his camel to continue the journey, he wrote this last letter for the Cooks to preserve in their archives. 'Gentlemen,—Before leaving for Berber

I would wish to express to you my own and Lieut.-Colonel Stewart's thanks for the admirable manner in which we have been treated while on your steamers. Your agents have also on every occasion shown themselves kind and obliging, and have in every way assisted us to the best of their ability. Hoping that I may perhaps again have the pleasure of placing myself under your guidance, I remain, ever yours truly: (Signed) C. E. GORDON, Major-General and Governor-General.'

CHAPTER TWENTY-ONE

The Nile Expert

THE hesitant tactics in Khartoum, and the dilatory strategies of Cairo and London which culminated in the violent death of Charles Gordon, described by Gladstone as 'the hero of heroes,' are not within the province of this story which must concern itself with ways and means rather than with policies. As far as John Mason Cook was concerned, the sequel to Gordon's letter was a summons, only a few weeks later, to the Admiralty in London. The military and naval authorities needed his advice in planning an expedition to extricate Gordon and Stewart from Khartoum. During the subsequent 'months of fatal indecision,' as Lord Cromer called them, Cook continued to give what advice he could. Not the least of the difficulties was lack of proper information about whole stretches of the Nile in the Nubian Desert. The map the planners were using had been drawn in 1831. It not only showed the Third Cataract as being at Hannek, where there proved to be nothing more than a rapid, but also omitted altogether four or five cataracts which lay between Wady Halfa and Hannek. Naval surveyors had recently been sent to report on the river, but they had done so at a season of high water and their observations had failed to reveal the true state of affairs.

Cook attended meeting after meeting, giving what

advice he could, based on his sixteen years' knowledge of
working the river. The outcome was that he contracted to
carry the whole expedition. He was told there would be
6,000 men and 10,000 tons of stores. There were also
400 whale boats which were to be carried by rail from
Alexandria to Assiout and thence towed to Wady Halfa by
steamer. Upon his initial estimates, Parliament voted
£600,000 to cover the cost of this; but as the months went
by the scheme grew in magnitude. The Admiralty said
that 12,000 tons of coal would be needed—which by some
mischance seems to have been omitted from their original
estimate. The War Office decided they needed more men,
more stores and more boats. In the end, the accounts show
that Cook was responsible for the conveyance of some
11,000 English and 7,000 Egyptian troops, 130,000 tons
of stores and war material and 800 whale boats.

The Admiralty's afterthought about coal proved to
be modest; 70,000 tons were in fact needed, and Cook
used 28 large steamers running between the Tyne and
Alexandria, 6,000 trucks on the Egyptian railways, 27
steamers running day and night on the Nile, and 650
sailing vessels to move it. Despite the fact that he ordered
20,000 tons to be sent from the Tyne to Egypt so that it
arrived before he had even signed his own contract with
the Government, there were insinuations in a subsequent
report that the cumbersome expedition which took so long
to plan had been impeded by lack of coal; a charge which
Cook with good justification hotly denied.

He seems to have left the conference tables of London
just as soon as his task had been agreed in principle. From
his own story of the affair (which fortunately has been
preserved in some detail as he recounted it to fellow
members of the Royal Geographical Society afterwards
and printed in pamphlet form a lecture he gave elsewhere),
it is clear that he wasted no time in throwing himself into
the mechanics of the job on the spot. He did not limit his
activities to armchair work in Cairo but hastened south

along the Nile, with some courage and much resourcefulness to see what would really confront this movement
of a waterborne army through a desert. It is clear that he
himself in the first place had no idea of the difficulties
which would be encountered in forcing the expedition
through to the Upper Nile. Dongola, then almost unknown
Nubian territory, had been selected as the point of
concentration from which the relieving force would make
its advance on Khartoum. Cook's trek thither to explore
the many difficulties the expedition would encounter, was,
to say the least of it, an uncomfortable venture for a
specialist in the comforts of travel. Though his journey
was practical rather than political, he gained an interview with the local potentate, the Moudir of Dongola,
Mahommed Ahmed, who earlier had proclaimed himself
the Mahdi of the Sudan, but had since been rejected as
a false prophet. Cook found the Moudir squatting on
a chair with another chair before him bearing papers
and an ink-pad for his seal. His holy spear was at his
side.

'Tell Mr. Cook, Mahommed Ahmed is no Mahdi,' he
said through an interpreter. 'There is no Mahdi. If there
were a Mahdi, I should be the one—but I am not. Tell
Mr. Cook I invite him to rest here a fortnight. At the end
of that time I will send him with an escort to Khartoum.'

Whether the false Mahdi, who had formerly worked as
a shipbuilder really recognized the much-travelled name
of Cook, or whether he fancied that the unassuming but
prosperous business man before him had come to play
some vital part in the affairs of the Sudan will never be
known. His suggestion of a safe conduct to Khartoum was,
to say the least of it, astonishing to one who had been
laboriously checking the possibilities of getting a relieving
force through to Gordon. 'Here was England spending a
few millions to rescue Gordon from Khartoum,' said Cook
afterwards, 'and here was a gentleman who offered to
send me there in a fortnight.'

He tried not to move a muscle and he said: 'Ask His Excellency whether he considers it would be perfectly safe to go to Khartoum in a fortnight.'

'Certainly,' came the reply, 'with my escort, in a fortnight; the road will be perfectly clear and there will be no obstacle.'

'Ask His Excellency why Gordon cannot come away from Khartoum.'

Mahommed Ahmed pushed back his turban. 'Ask Mr. Cook, if Gordon leaves Khartoum, who is to govern there . . .'

Cook knew his limitations, and his terms of reference. Even his genius for organization would be of little use to Gordon. Khartoum needed soldiers, not civilian organizers, however skilful. 'I came away,' he said, 'impressed with the idea that I had had a conversation with one of the ablest and cleverest men I had ever seen'—and Cook had pitted his resources against able and clever men during a long business life. He reported back to Lord Wolseley, drawing attention to the worst of the navigational hazards, and much too late, through no fault of his, the expedition set out.

His story must be told in the reported speech, for such is the only record of his address to the Royal Geographical Society: 'It was a succession of great difficulties, and in all his travelling experience and his contact with military movements, nothing had pleased him more than to work day by day by the side of our soldiers on the river, especially the Staffordshire Regiment, which was the pioneer regiment, and had to find out the channels and difficulties for those who were following them. He was near that regiment almost the whole of the time they were working their way up. The soldiers had had no previous experience whatever in river work, but they worked most freely and willingly in trying circumstances, and pushed along whistling and singing to keep their spirits up, and it was certainly a most interesting sight. . . . In many points there was very shallow and rapid water. From Sarras to Sakarmatta, a distance of 74 miles, the rise was 450 feet as near as he could ascertain by his aneroid. He himself travelled in the most favourable circumstances, having the assistance of the Egyptian troops, and his was the only boat, except whalers, that succeeded in getting through from the Lower Nile to Dongola. Even the pinnaces were not able to go up the whole distance. His boat was only twenty-four feet long, six feet six inches beam, drawing only twenty inches of water, yet at different points it required 170 men, in addition to his own crew, to pull it through the cataracts, and at one point seventy-five Dongolese had to be employed in addition. That would give some idea of the troubles that our soldiers had to encounter. . . . The men were in splendid health. Of course they suffered the first few days, especially from blisters, having to walk on parched granite rocks tugging at their boats, which were moved along some days only one or two miles, while for five consecutive days his glass registered ninety degrees in the shade, and was scarcely below eighty degrees at night. . . .

'. . . Considerable difference of opinion had prevailed as to the wisdom of sending out the whalers and the Canadian boatmen. When he was asked his opinion he said it was not necessary to send out whalers, and that he could find plenty of boats in the country to work out the expedition. He also thought then that it was not necessary to send out Canadian boatmen, because sufficient natives could be found to do the work, but he was bound to admit now that in that opinion he was wrong. The necessary boats could not have been found in the Upper Nile, and it would have been impossible to conduct the expedition as far as Dongola by the river without the assistance of European boats. At least half the Canadians sent out were the finest boatmen he had ever come in contact with, and he was satisfied that the work they did, and the impetus they gave to the other men, would fully repay the Government for the cost of conveying them from Canada to Egypt. After ascending the seventy-four miles he made up his mind that no power whatever would induce him in any circumstances to come down the Nile through the cataracts and rapids that he had worked up, but there again he had to give way, and he did come down the Nile in one of the whalers. He and his son passed through the whole of the cataracts of Dal, Akasha, Tangor, Ambigol, and Semneh, and he felt as comfortable and as much at his ease after he had passed through the first cataract as he did when sitting in his own easy chair in his library. After he saw the manner in which the Canadians steered through the first cataract, he was perfectly satisfied that he need not trouble himself any more, and he accomplished in little over eleven hours the distance which took him thirteen days on the upward journey, though in the latter case he had all the assistance that the Egyptian army and Government officials could give him. . . .

'The question naturally arose, how many boats had been lost, and how many lives had been lost, by capsizing? Up to the time when he left Sarras, which was about 12th December, the whole of the 800 boats, with the exception of about forty or fifty, had left Sarras, and he had met them at different points on the river. He saw one only entirely wrecked. Through a misunderstanding, arising from the differences of language, a Dongolese crew let go at the most inopportune moment, and the boat went down the cataract and was broken almost straight in two. That was the only whaler up to that time that had been capsized with any serious injury. Some days his boat could not go half an hour without striking on some rock, and although it had timbers an inch and a half thick, he had to take it out of the water several times to have it repaired. On one occasion there were twenty holes knocked in it at one cataract, and two days were required to repair it. He supposed that about one hundred boats were injured, but only in such a way that the men could repair them in a short time; and as a rule they were in the water again ready to go forward within an hour or two. A few lives had been lost, among them seven of the Canadians, but he believed if the matter were investigated it would be found that these Canadians were not real boatmen; they were men who were not accustomed to the working of boats. Five soldiers had been lost, one of them through getting on the wrong side of the rope; he was pulled into the cataract and carried away. He saw several of the soldiers fall into the habit of the natives of stripping themselves naked and pushing the boats, and one soldier who did so was carried away by an undercurrent. The loss of life had been remarkably small, and he was only surprised that hundreds of lives had not been sacrificed.'

Here I must not pursue the fortunes of the men, but that of some of the boats that carried them. The Nile steamers belonging to the Egyptian Government were casualties of the war. They were worn-out and no longer fit for the tourist traffic that was ready to flock back to the river. Cook was forced to surrender them together with his concessions, for the Egyptians were unwilling or unable to rehabilitate them.

There followed the boldest decision of Cook's business life. He would build a fleet of his own. Once again he abandoned the policy of agency for that of ownership. He bought land at Boulac for his own shipyard. By the final decade of the century, his contracts renewed with both the British and Egyptian Governments, Cook enjoyed an official and lucrative monopoly over much of the Nile. On a grand social occasion in 1890, the Khedive of Egypt, who had decorated John Mason Cook and two of his sons, insisted upon being the first to inspect the *Rameses the Great*, the most splendid steamer the Nile had ever seen. It had been prefabricated on the Clyde and re-assembled at the Boulac works. In one of the many speeches that marked the occasion, Cook recalled that

when he had made his first trip to the Nile, twenty years
before, there had been only one passenger-carrying steamer
and 136 dahabeahs (a sort of sailing barge or houseboat).
Now there were fifteen steamers all running under his
ownership and not more than thirty dahabeahs.

The heyday of the Cook steamers was pleasantly
recalled for me when I picked up in a second-hand book-
shop a work* by the travel-writer and one-time editor of
Who's Who, Douglas Sladen, published at the beginning
of the present century. In his preface, the writer confesses
that he is 'entirely at a loss' how to express his indebted-
ness to the firm of Cook. 'There seems to be no limit to
the influence of this firm in Egypt. All the way up the
river, I found my path smoothed for me by letters from
their General Manager . . .' Whether or not his revealing
chapter entitled *With Cook in Egypt* was intended as a *quid
pro quo*, I have not been able to discover. Whatever may
have been its early purpose I have found it a charming
period piece, nostalgically reflecting more spacious and
leisurely things. A few of us who served in the Middle East
in World War II were lucky enough to use some of the
old Cook steamers that had been taken over both by
the Army and the R.A.F. as waterfront billets in Cairo.
Coming from canvas to spend a few nights in what
seemed at that time the height of luxury afloat, I often
used to wonder about the former glories of the old
steamers. Quite by accident I found the answer in
Sladen.

He admired the large cabins with beds so high above
the floor that an American saratoga would go under them.
He grumbled a little because the electric light was cut off
at eleven at night, curtailing your leisure to read all the
best books on Egypt which were carried in the ship's
library. There was a cosy little reading-room and the
newspapers arrived on board every day. Mail was cleared
every night and you found your letters beside your plate

* *Egypt and the English* (Hurst and Blackett, 1908).

at breakfast, 'just as you would at home.' That breakfast was 'a country house meal,' starting with porridge, proceeding with 'bacon and eggs and fish and other hot dishes and ham and tongue and chicken and other cold fare, to jam and marmalade.' It needed to be a hearty meal for you could not help getting up early when there was 'an Egyptian sunrise mingling heaven and earth and the waking life of the villages to watch.'

Mornings and afternoons might be occupied by sight-seeing or by excursions. The social centre was the lounge on the promenade deck, 'awninged above from the sun by day, and awninged all round at night till it looks like a marquee put up for a ball. As it is full of easy chairs and tea-tables and windscreens, the idle and the unintelligent lounge about it all day long when they are not making excursions (which they like for the donkey rides), reading novels, or dozing, or playing bridge. Their day begins with afternoon tea, at which you have half Huntley and Palmer's productions instead of bread and butter. Special friends make up tea-parties, and the beautiful Arab servants, in white robes and bright red tarbooshes, sashes and slippers, glide about, filling up the tea-cups as fast as they are emptied and bringing fresh varieties of Huntley and Palmer to compel people to over-eat themselves. This goes playfully on till somebody discovers that sunset is beginning. Then even the least intelligent people on the ship hurry to the side, not for the usual reason, and bring up ejaculations for a solid hour while the Egyptian sky proceeds with its marvellous transformation-scenes.'

I hope I may be forgiven over-much quotation in offering this last glimpse of the social life that Cook created and that our contemporary Cook-booked, jet-propelled air passengers have left behind for ever: 'In the height of the season, when the tourist steamers are full, on the days when there are no excursions, the particular young man sometimes breaks out into silk suits and wonderful socks, or, at any rate, rare and irreproachable flannels, just as

the girl who has come to conquer Cairo society rings the
gamut of summer extravagances. They have the moral
courage for at least two different costumes between
breakfast and dinner; and though a mere man is limited
to his theatre jacket for dinner, the irresponsible girl can
dress as elaborately as she pleases for the evening, and
the climate tempts her. . . . By dinner-time most people
are tired—tired of doing nothing if there has been no
excursion; tired of long rides over the hot Desert, and hard
sightseeing, if there has been an excursion. They sit down
with great content to a good dinner, and when it is over
move out to the marquee which has been improvised out
of the lounge for their coffee and cigarettes and a little
light chatter; and, if they are wise, read their guide-books.
On our steamer nobody played bridge except the two
clergymen and their wives.'

The Cooks' Nile fleet sailed happily on throughout the
'twenties and 'thirties of this century, most of them carrying
a European manager, a doctor, and a chef whose catering
compared favourably with that of ocean-going liners.
During World War I they were commandeered for
military service. During World War II most of them
remained immobilized in the vicinity of Cairo, and thus
many Middle East veterans will remember them. Afterwards they were sold and among their new owners was
Ali Maher Pasha, who lived aboard the *Memnon* before
becoming Prime Minister of Egypt.

The works which John Mason Cook created at Boulac
as a shipbuilding and servicing yard for his Nile steamers
developed into one of the most important engineering
undertakings in Egypt, possessing the largest floating dock
on the Nile. In peace-time its work outgrew its original
scope of steamer maintenance. What had originally been
intended as an expedient side-line of the Cook tourism
grew out of all proportion into an independent self-
supporting industrial branch. Its activities included public
works contracts such as water-boring and installation of

fresh-water supplies to villages, generating plants, overhead
electric cables, water-towers, pipe-lines and even passenger
elevators, besides many contracts undertaken for the
British armed forces, the Egyptian Government and
industrial firms. With World War II Boulac expanded to
serve the Middle East forces. Motor torpedo boats were
built for the Admiralty. Portable kitchens, wireless cars,
mobile photographic dark-rooms and ambulances were
built for the Army. Eight hundred men were employed
recovering and rehabilitating the hardworked vehicles of
the Desert Army. It was a far cry from the war activities
of John Mason Cook. Yet the existence of such a plant in
Egypt was, I think, a tribute to the foresight of that
undaunted spirit who built with such energy and yet
planned with such flexibility when global wars were
unknown.

The influence of the Cooks in Egypt was wholly good.
They brought trade and they found employment for large
numbers of the Egyptians. At Luxor a well-equipped
hospital was caused to be built by Thomas Cook out of
the subscriptions of his clients—a notable example of his
power of doing good by proxy.

Even *Blackwood's Magazine*, which had promoted earlier
criticisms of Cook's tours in Italy, printed a not unkindly
word by G. W. Steevens on the subject of Cook: 'The
nominal suzerain of Egypt is the Sultan; its real suzerain
is Lord Cromer. Its nominal Governor is the Khedive; its
real governor, for a final touch of comic opera, is Thomas
Cook & Son. Cook's representative is the first person you
meet in Egypt, and you go on meeting him. He sees you
in; he sees you through; he sees you out. You see the back
of a native turban, long blue gown, red girdle, bare brown
legs; "How truly oriental!" you say. Then he turns round,
and you see "Cook's Porter" emblazoned across his breast.
"You travel Cook, sir," he grins; "all right." And it is all
right. Cook carries you, like a nursing father, from one end
of Egypt to the other. Cook has personally conducted

more than one expedition into the Sudan, and done it as no Transport Department could do. The population of the Nile banks raises produce for Cook, and for him alone. In other countries, the lower middle-classes aspire to a place under Government; in Egypt they aspire to a place under Cook. "Good Cook shop all the time," is the native's giddiest ambition—a permanent engagement with Cook.'

CHAPTER TWENTY-TWO

The Family and the World

TRUE to its sturdy Midland origin, and typical of its own solid times, Cook's remained a family concern. Even now, almost a quarter of a century since any of the Cook family have participated in the affairs of the firm, long-serving members of the staff, without any false sentiment, like to think of it as a family business, untrammelled by red tape or remote control by the State. John Mason Cook had been an active junior partner to his father for many years before he was formally admitted as such in 1878. By that time the two men seemed to have arrived at an uncomplicated formula for sharing the work between them. Both were pioneers and imbued with a zeal for good causes, but while the father, particularly at the outset of his career, had seen his travel activities as only part of a comprehensive pattern of progressive reform, the son seems inclined to have subdued all else to the business of travel. His own sons, as we have seen, equipped with some of the languages their elders lacked, were soon playing their useful parts in the pattern, though, as the organization grew and spread, there was naturally a tendency for the younger men to specialize geographically or departmentally.

The home life of the Cooks, on the face of it, might be expected to have been hectic and complicated. But both men seemed to have possessed a national tranquility, not by any means bereft of gusto. They were far from being stay-at-homes; but theirs was the ample family life of the go-ahead business man of their times which demanded the utmost of men whose capital was their brains. Preaching, printing, self-improvement, propaganda, self-help, social progress—that was just the right background for such people. There was nothing restless about it. The only survivor of the third generation, Mr. Ernest E. Cook, assures me that in the various homes that John Mason's family occupied in South London and the nearer suburbs, there was never any sense of haste or disruption. It was taken as a matter of course that the father and the grand-father travelled extensively; but their comings and goings were never so sudden or prolonged that the children felt denied a natural relationship.

The Thomas Cooks used the Bloomsbury Street boarding-house when they stayed in London, but London was never their home. Mrs. Thomas Cook continued to supervise the London boarding-house and the Leicester hotel until 1879 when both establishments were let off. Thereafter the Thomas Cooks moved to Thorncroft, a roomy, red-brick house in London Road, then on the outskirts of Leicester. This was considered a palatial abode by many of Cook's former associates, and some still living look back upon its galleried hall with dining, breakfast, drawing-rooms and library with something like awe.

One of these is Mr. Alfred H. Bishop, son of the minister of the Archdeacon Lane Baptist Church where the Cook family worshipped. Characteristically, Cook frequently took his minister with him on trips abroad, to the Scilly Isles, France, Scotland and the Holy Land, and also to America and Canada to preach as he went. Mr. Bishop's memories give us glimpses of Thomas Cook at Thorncroft in the proper setting of all his modest glory, the provincial returned from the ends of the earth to enjoy a Midland hearth. 'Mr. Cook loved to have friends round him at the Festive Season. There was a long table in the Dining Room, generally full to capacity on Christmas Day. My father was always given the job of carving the turkey (of prodigious size) at one end of the table and generally one of the Mason family was at the other end to carve the huge sirloin of beef. Father had the worst of it as everyone seemed to prefer turkey. We boys used afterwards to be allowed to play at puss-in-the-corner in the Hall with some of the younger guests and I seem to remember in the early days Mr. Cook coming out of the Drawing Room to watch benevolently as we enjoyed the game.'

Lest it be thought that Cook turned Pickwickian in his declining years, here is a recollection of his many Leicester Sundays: 'His kind benevolent face was usually either placid or smiling, and no doubt to my eyes when I first knew him he seemed older than he really was. He used on Sundays to sit in the back seat of Archdeacon Lane Chapel and he had a habit of putting his hands together and twirling his thumbs one over the other during the whole time he was listening to the sermon. I have no memory of his doing it at other times, though he may have done so. He was a regular attendant on Sundays and after he went to live at Thorncroft, he had a closed-in carriage, something like a glorified small bus (without top seats of course), with a seat down each side. The cushions were covered with blue cloth and when Mr. Cook called at our house to take mother down to chapel, as he sometimes did, I used occasionally to get a ride, and when this happened, I felt myself to be a very grand and fortunate person.'

Mrs. Thomas Cook is recollected by all who knew her as a small, trim figure, with a business brain at least a match for her husband's. During the early excursion days, she often accompanied him on trips to Scotland and Ireland. In later years she did not hesitate to venture across the Channel. Many of her journeys abroad were religious. When Cook was instrumental in starting the first Baptist Mission to Rome in 1873, for instance, she and her daughter spent two or three weeks preparing the new chapel for worship. That only daughter of theirs, Annie Elizabeth, helped with the hotel businesses and also in supervising the domestic side of those ventures which the Cooks ran in London and Paris for Exhibition tourists. It was a cruel stroke that she should have been a victim of domestic improvement.

One of the wonders in its time was the gas water-heater installed by Thomas Cook in his bathroom at Thorncroft. But on the first Saturday evening after it was fitted, Annie Elizabeth, returning from a Women's Sewing Class to enjoy this new comfort, was overcome by gas fumes from the new apparatus, fell back and was drowned in the bath. To her memory, Thomas Cook erected, at a cost of £7,000, in the Italian style, a memorial hall and classrooms for the Sunday school she had served for seventeen years. It stood at the corner of Archdeacon Lane and Orchard Street, then a residential district, and a centre of non-conformist activity, but one which, alas, subsequently 'went down.' In 1937 it was scheduled as a slum clearance area, and during World War II Annie's memorial was being used as a warehouse. In 1946 the Charity Commissioners offered the property for sale at £4,000. It was acquired for demolition by the Corporation of Leicester.

Apart from its single tragic incident, the Cook domestic scene, then, was little different in its unsullied respectability from that of many a family emerging from the Industrial Revolution to enjoy the substantial dream of late-Victorian England. They feared God. They stuck to their principles. They enlarged the family circle. They promoted the family business. Such is the unexceptional background to that methodical vision and ardent opportunism of theirs that was 'limited only by the boundaries of the habitable globe.'

The family aspect of it all was evidently regarded with a certain amount of scepticism even in the 'nineties when Fraser Rae mentions rumours that had been current for a decade that Cook's were 'American speculators,' that there were 'no Cooks in the business,' and that Americans persisted in a delusion that Thomas Cook & Son was a title of a very large joint stock company. Americans, he tells us, sometimes showed astonishment at meeting John Mason Cook, being quite convinced that there could be no personification to match the legend. Rae stresses the fact that the capital of the business was provided exclusively by the partners 'while the third generation consists of the three sons of Mr. John Mason Cook and they have been carefully trained to carry on . . . in the future.' There was Frank Henry Cook, whom we have already met as a youngster in the Near East which he loved and who by the 'nineties had first-hand experience also of America and India. There was Ernest E. Cook who made an exploratory visit with his brother Frank in the Caucasus and Persia before going on by himself to the Antipodes. In after years he preferred to specialize in the financial side of the business, and since his retirement in the late 'twenties has lived in Bath. The third son, Thomas Albert, joined his brothers in taking over the business when the reign of John Mason came to its end, and he remained with the firm until after World War I.

Both Thomas Cook and his son, so placid domestically, were in their work most gifted opportunists, always ready to serve any sudden event in war or in peace. An astonishing diversity of events and people carried them abroad to the unlikeliest destinations. Fraser Rae, living closer in time to his hero, felt impelled to defend this opportunism. Whether they were envious minds or merely business rivals who found in Thomas Cook a sanctimonious subject for reproach, I cannot discover. Certainly his Victorian biographer, ever ready to rush to the defence of the Cook name and capital, went to some pains over principles. 'He started in the business which he had made his own without any capital more tangible than his brains, and without any other support than that which might accrue from the exercise of his faculties. Though his work was philanthropic in the best sense of the term, it could not be carried on unless a profit were to be made. As a labourer he was as deserving of reward as any other, and when his business increased the pecuniary reward did not tarry. . . . When Mr. Thomas Cook was reproached with making a commercial speculation of his business, he was able to retort that no business could be conducted except upon business principles.'

Let us now return to Thomas Cook himself in the years where we left him, before the pecuniary rewards were quite so assured, when the milk and honey of the Middle East had only just been tasted. He had been east and west and there remained his 'crowning achievement,' as he always liked to describe it—the girdling of the globe. In 1872, he was already enough of a public figure for this project to interest the Editor of *The Times*. When Cook set out for his exploratory trip with nine companions of mixed nationality, including Scottish, Russians and Americans, he recorded his impressions in a series of letters, some of which were printed in *The Times*. He subsequently printed them in a book entitled *Letters from the Sea and from Foreign Lands—description of a Tour Round the Globe*—a volume which was published by the firm, sold at a shilling, and carried detailed advertisements of all Cook's arrangements. 'This going round the world is a very easy and almost imperceptible business . . .' he wrote with his usual relish—in spite of the fact that the initial voyage to New York in the *Oceanic* in bad weather took thirteen days.

He was not out to set records but to learn 'with perfect accuracy the best way round the globe,'—and by that he meant the best way round for the greatest number of people. After five days' pause in New York, the party went to Niagara, then devoted three days to Chicago, at that time being rebuilt after the fire. They stopped at Salt Lake City long enough to observe the Silver Rush. Then they sailed by way of San Francisco to Yokohama, during which voyage Cook noted 'but for the discrepancies of watches, . . . we should not realize our approach to the meridian line or suppose it possible that the next land we see will be that of the rising sun.' They passed by way of Shanghai, Singapore and Ceylon to India, thence they returned through Aden and the Suez, Palestine, Turkey and Greece to England after a journey of two hundred and twenty-two days. Cook had not hurried, but his timing was perfect. *The Times* in London were printing his descriptive letters, *Le Temps* in Paris was running a serial by Jules Verne. It was called *Voyage autour de monde en quatre-vingt jours*. Eighty days! A gallic exaggeration, of course, but how the story caught on! And here was Thomas Cook, returned to prove that such a journey, given time, was feasible enough, and ready as always to provide a ticket.

Early in this century few took to the round trip more eagerly than the Japanese. No sooner was a Cook office opened in Japen in 1908 than fifty-seven customers foregathered, all bent, as the travel literature said, upon enlarging the mind, widening the outlook on life and cultivating the taste. They got their money's-worth when they reached London, where they created almost as much sensation as Thomas Cook's band-led excursionists had done in Scotland sixty years previously. They were received at London's Mansion House and at the Guildhall. They were entertained by Members of Parliament to tea on the terrace of the House of Commons, and by Lord Northcliffe to a garden party arranged in their honour.

So those readers of Verne's international best-seller who could afford the time and money took their globe-trotting inclinations to Cooks. Until the end of World War I, they crossed America by rail. Afterwards there was a wealthy vogue for world cruises by liner. Just before World War II there were Cook advertisements offering a less leisurely generation circumnavigation of the globe in thirty days by air.

CHAPTER TWENTY-THREE

Pilgrims and Princes

WITH Victoria proclaimed Empress in 1877, came the heyday of the Anglo-Indian. The Cooks had spread their systems over Europe, America, Australia and the Middle East. They had learned 'with perfect accuracy the best way round the globe.' The Suez Canal was still young: its potential was plain. No wonder John Mason Cook hastened to India in 1880 to survey exciting new prospects. 'His father and himself were of opinion that, while it would be well to arrange for the visits of Englishmen to India, it would be even more serviceable if the wealthy natives of India would be induced to visit Europe,' goes the official record.

The Queen Empress and the more sophisticated pleasures of Europe were to provide inducement in plenty. It is not for nothing that the Cook Headquarters still maintains its *Eastern Princes Dept.* John Mason's journey was a fair example of that inspired opportunism, of being in the right place at the right time. Moreover, the Cooks had sufficiently progressed in the world to invoke the blessing of a Prime Minister. They had sought no favours in forty years. The mission to India, however, was a matter of national importance, worthy, they thought, of Gladstone's support.

The great man was cordial. 'Your proposals well

deserve the most favourable consideration that circumstances will permit, on account of the real public value which attaches to your successful efforts for promoting intercommunication between countries.'

The outcome was a letter from the Marquess of Hartington: 'The Secretary of State for India is disposed to regard with favour any plan which would embrace arrangements on reasonable terms between yourself and the Indian Government, or the Indian guaranteed companies to facilitate railway travelling in India and add to the convenience and comfort of passengers.'

Though Prime Minister Gladstone was an ally (and indeed a customer), the younger Cook was shrewd enough to allow for the frailties of party politics, and he sought the favour also of the Marquess of Salisbury, the former Minister then in opposition, who obligingly wrote: 'Mr. Cook, I do not hesitate to say that the Government ought to render you every possible assistance to enable you to carry out your ideas, as it is impossible to calculate what benefit you will ultimately be to the nation. If you can only induce a number of wealthy Englishmen to visit India, and see for themselves the value of that country to England, and also induce even a small number of the wealthy Indians to visit England, and enable them to realize who and what the people are at home who govern them in India, you will certainly be of great service from a social and international point of view, and, it may be, politically.'

Thus armed, Cook established himself by opening offices in Bombay and Calcutta, appointing representatives in other parts and arranging for international tickets over the whole Indian railway system. No sooner was this typically efficient consolidation carried out, than he was faced with a new proposition, as unexpected as it was arduous, the reorganization of the hitherto scandalous pilgrim traffic to Mecca.

The Cooks, it must be noticed in passing, though their

Baptist and temperance ardour never diminished, had not
been dismayed by business transactions with people of
other persuasions either in religion or drink. Only a year
or so before the Governor-General of India, the Earl of
Dufferin, approached him about the Mecca pilgrims, Cook
had conveyed a party of French Roman Catholic pilgrims,
a thousand strong, through the Holy Land to Jerusalem.
Even though the French Government had given him
an official warning that the exploit was, in their view,
dangerous, most of the party being under canvas, Cook
had completed his task without a hitch and without
religious scruple. A member of the Cook staff, H. H.
Spiller, a few years later conducted across the Channel the
first Roman Catholic pilgrimage ever to leave England
since the Reformation, a party of one thousand two
hundred people led by the Duke of Norfolk. No wonder
then that there is a Pilgrimages Department to be found
in the Cook headquarters at the present day.

In the 'eighties, when Cook, newly established in India
to seek quite other trade, was asked to tackle the problem
of the Mohammedan pilgrims to the shrine of their
Prophet in Arabia, he knew that he was undertaking a
task which was new to his experience and one that many
others had turned down. 'I know that this business,' he
wrote, 'is surrounded with more difficulties and prejudices
than anything I have hitherto undertaken.'

The pilgrims, a majority of them subjects of the Queen-
Empress, were not only paying extortionate rates for their
transport but suffering such hardship on the journey from
the ports of India to the Hejaz that the lives of many of
them had been endangered. Mecca, where a mongrel
population of sixty thousand was mostly engaged in
pillaging the faithful, had no drainage system, its water
supply dated from the sixteenth century, and slave traffic
throve. It was beyond the powers of the Indian Government or of Cook to remedy these conditions. But the over-
crowding, squalor, distress and extortion of the journey

across India and by sea to Jidda, scandalously mismanaged by hordes of long-vested interests, was an overdue reform calling for immediate action. The Cook experience was officially called upon to solve what we have now learned to call a problem of logistics. Cook, taking his younger son, Thomas Albert, as assistant, travelled thousands of miles, meeting inertia, pessimism and fierce opposition. He was armed with his own shrewdness and patience and also with a firm directive from the Government: 'The Governor-General in Council feels convinced that a scheme of the nature above described cannot fail, if successfully carried out, to be productive of much benefit to Indian pilgrims to the Hejaz; but if success is to be ensured, it is essential that every assistance should be afforded to Messrs. Cook & Son, not only by local governments and administrations, but also by district and other officers upon whom it will devolve to give effect to the detailed arrangements. His Excellency in Council accordingly trusts that local governments and administrations will see that this is done, and will direct local officers to co-operate in every possible manner with the representatives of the firm in carrying out their operations.'

A copy of this document was displayed in all administrative offices and published in the Press throughout India; but it took more than that to subdue the violence of those who made a living out of the pilgrims. The terms of reference were comprehensive. As the Government agent, Cook was responsible for all transport from the shores of India to Jidda and back. He was to receive assistance from officials throughout India. One of the firm's tickets was to be issued to each pilgrim by the Government Office providing the passport. The Pilgrimage Office in Bombay was placed under the control of Cook with responsibility directly to the Government. 'Thomas Cook & Son are to arrange with the railway administrations, steamship proprietors, etc., etc., for the conveyance of the pilgrims, quoting through fares from all chief stations in India to

A COOK POSTER AT THE TURN OF THE CENTURY

DONALD WHITE, A FAMOUS COOK COURIER, WITH ONE OF THE NEW LADY COURIERS

Jidda and return; they are to do everything they can to secure the proper transit in satisfactory ships, with proper accommodation in accordance with the regulations laid down in the manual issued by the Government, and to do their utmost to meet all the present objectionable features in precisely the same manner as they conduct the other parts of their business.'

With authority and his usual quiet and stubborn energy, Cook cleaned up the business. The Cook name was carried to the remotest corners of India. Recognition came from the Khedive and from many Pashas and Sheikhs of the Mohammedan world. The prestige value was gratifying, but the younger Cook never let idealism run away with his sense of reality, and he noted soberly that it all proved to be more a labour of love 'than he had counted upon.'

Nevertheless, there was consolation in the Indian traffic that followed it, the almost fabulous journeys of the Indian Princes, Maharajahs and Potentates to pay homage to the Imperial Throne and to taste the pleasures of Europe. It began when J. M. Cook was officially asked to make the travel arrangements for the Indian Princes attending the Queen-Empress's Jubilee celebrations in London in 1887. It still goes on. The processional splendours of the English aristocrats who made the Grand Tour before the Cooks threw Europe open to the multitude, pale beside the splendours of these customers who for three-quarters of a century have made their progresses from the East. In contrast with the meagre needs of the Mecca pilgrims, Cook found himself dealing with individual requirements of unique prodigality. A prince desiring a conducted tour of Europe requested that the arrangements should include for 200 servants, 50 family attendants and 20 chefs. His impedimenta included 10 elephants, 33 tame tigers, 1,000 packing-cases and a small howitzer from the Royal Palace.

For some racy accounts of the style of some of these most opulent of all Cook's tourists, I am indebted to Mr. G.

H

Piccoli who retired from the Cook office in Rome in 1951. His first encounter was in 1905, when he met the Maharajah of Baroda who arrived at Naples by specially-chartered steamer. His Highness desired to have a hotel to himself, so the Hotel Royal was acquired for his party, which included cows and sheep which had to be accommodated in the small garden attached to the hotel. All beds had to be removed as the party slept upon their own air mattresses and all pictures had to be taken down. All meals were prepared by Indian cooks, who milked the cows and killed the sheep in the garden.

Closer to our times, came the Nawab of Rampur, who arrived in Rome in the mid-'thirties and demanded that the Cook office should arrange for the Military Cavalry School to give a riding show in order to satisfy a bet which His Highness had made with one of his friends on Italian equitation. Mr. Piccoli modestly describes this as 'a request out of the ordinary.' Imbued with something of the spirit of the founders of his organization, he interviewed an Italian General and persuaded him to summon by telegram all the officers of the school who at that time were away on leave. The show took place five days after the Nawab's arrival and His Highness was so well satisfied that he bought from Mappin & Webb twenty-five gold watches which were engraved for presentation to the officers and, very properly, to Mr. Piccoli himself.

There were fantastic interludes with Indian excursionists even as recently as 1939. A certain Prince arrived in Rome in the August of that year with a family and suite numbering forty-five. This Prince, Piccoli learned from a secretary who had come in advance, expected 'a big fuss' to be made—with soldiers, flowers, a red carpet and an official reception. The Man from Cook's did his best. He obtained from the municipal authorities half a dozen policemen in uniform. From the Grand Hotel he borrowed a red carpet which was rolled down from the train to the station exit. He persuaded the Chief Stationmaster to

welcome the Prince and for flowers to be offered to the
royal ladies. From the entire floor of the Grand Hotel
that were his quarters, His Highness declared that he
wished for an audience with the King, the Duce and the
Pope during the course of his week's stay. Victor Emmanuel
and Mussolini were out of Rome and the Pope was at his
summer residence at Castelgandolfo. His Highness settled
for the Pope.

But there was the complication that he wished to take
for his audience a small orchestra, a singer and a dancer,
in order to give a concert. The Man from Cook's was told
that the audience was possible but not the singing and
dancing. Undeterred, however, the entertainers were taken
along, together with an ivory crucifix by Gennaro Bernini,
procured by Cooks as a present from the Prince to the
Pope. His Highness made a long speech. His Holiness
replied in English. Then the tricky question of the
entertainment was approached. With admirable foresight,
the Man from Cook's had persuaded Monsignor Casimiri
of the Sistine Choir to rehearse the players in the Vatican
Hymn. This they performed shakily but with great verve,
and followed with a programme of Indian songs which His
Holiness duly applauded.

This created a new problem for the hard-pressed Mr.
Piccoli. The Prince was so delighted with the performance
before the Holy Father that he demanded the use of a
theatre in Rome where the entertainment might be
repeated in public. Piccoli obtained the use for an afternoon of the Teatro della Arti and sent out invitations to
members of Roman society to fill it. Once more the Prince
and his performers received polite and seemly applause.

There were the usual calls for sightseeing and night
life. Then His Highness encountered a man with a parrot
and a see-saw. The parrot swung and whistled while the
man played and sang. For the rest of his stay, the Prince
found it difficult to dispense for long with this enchanting
company and much of Piccoli's time was taken up in

ensuring the presence of the performers. Even when the
Prince left by special train for Florence, they had to go
along too. 'Only when we were half way to Florence the
Prince got tired of him and gave orders for him to quit
the train. What could we do? It was a non-stop train so
the man had to remain quietly in a compartment until
Florence was reached.'

This was but one of the least of the problems confronting
the Man from Cook's during the Prince's journeys. 'When
we left Milan by special train for Switzerland, I noticed
that there was a member of the party missing. I made
enquiries to know who it was, but nobody would tell me.
I then asked the Prince, who said it was a relative
whom he did not want to see any more. He added that he
had locked him in the room at the Hotel, showing me the
key. I told the Prince that his relative being left in the
lurch, without any money, would have experienced a lot
of trouble—but he was determined to leave the man
behind. However, my colleague at Milan came to see us
en route, and I asked him to travel with us as far as the
frontier station, as I intended to tackle the Prince on the
subject. This was unsuccessful. At Domodossola, the Prince
handed over the key of the room, telling me to let the
relative join the party in Lucerne that evening.'

There was a sequel while they were attending a
Toscanini concert in Lucerne. 'Half-way through the
concert, one of his secretaries called to tell him that his
relative had arrived from Milan and had gone to bed. He
must have hated his relative, as he became so nervous
and furious, ordering me to get the man out of bed and
send him back to India. He also wanted one of his
secretaries to go back to India, as he had seen him asleep
on the train.

'I had no alternative but to go back to the Hotel
National, using all my persuasion to get the man ready to
leave that same evening for Genoa to embark on the
s.s. *Conte Grande* leaving for Bombay in about two or three

days. Luckily I found a double sleeping compartment for them, instructing the conductor to lock them up and hand them over to the Genoa Office, to whom I wrote a note to provide the necessary accommodation on the steamer, debiting the Prince's account with the expenses.'

Piccoli's final service to this distinguished Indian client was to escort him out of England after the declaration of war, another incident which is better told in his own words. 'When I went round to see the Prince at Grosvenor House there were two Englishmen, a doctor and an officer of the army, who had received instructions from the India Office to travel with the Prince as far as Suez and make sure that he would continue the voyage on to Bombay. I suggested travelling by air to Paris, as I had had a funny experience with mines in the Channel on my way over . . . The Prince listened to me and gave me *carte blanche* to arrange as suggested, whereas the doctor and officer preferred to go by steamer and meet us in Paris . . . During the flight the Prince tried to persuade me to remain in Paris for a week at least, but my orders were for a night only, which we spent at the Hotel Lotti. After reaching this Hotel, I asked instructions of the Prince what he wanted to do that evening. Reply was to have dinner at the Café de Paris at 8 o'clock and then go Chez Sheherazade, the Cabaret. Just before the time I went to his apartment to tell him that the cars were ready, but he could not be found. I enquired right and left to find out where he was, but nobody could tell me. But one of the hotel servants knew as he had provided a car for the Prince to go to an address in the Champs Elysées to see some lady friends. He would not tell me at first, but when I told him that he would not receive any backshish when we left the next day, he then disclosed the address, where I found him in conversation with two Parisian girls. I took him and the others to the Café de Paris, where I had ordered the supper. He wanted me to sit next to him, as he was always in the habit of asking questions all the time.

H*

We started with hors-d'œuvre and after a minute or two after we sat down I noticed him fast asleep with a piece of ham hanging down from his mouth. To wake him up I gave him a blow in the ribs. He opened his eyes asking what was the matter. I pointed out a lady who was dining at a table opposite saying that she was smiling at him. He immediately got up to see the lady, starting to dance with her round the room. The meal over we went to Sheherazade, where some champagne was served, pictures taken, and a dance or two. At ten o'clock, closing-time on account of the war, we left to return to the Hotel. The next day we left Paris in the evening by the Simplon Express for Venice, where the Prince and party embarked together with quite a number of horses and dogs bought in England for which I had to arrange for an escort to look after them on the voyage. The Prince wanted me to go all the way to Mysore, but I could not stay away so long from the Office, so I said good-bye to him and returned to Rome. He passed away a fortnight after his arrival in India.'

Oh, worthy shade of Thomas Cook! What strange worldly duties sometimes fall to the lot of your minions whose task it was to realize your dream that 'the wealthy natives of India should be induced to visit Europe.'

Certainly such social gambits were beyond imagination when Thomas Cook made his own visits to India and turned his attention to the red-jackets of the garrison. There were 5,908 abstainers, he had been told, in the Army in India. 'I have had the pleasure,' he wrote, 'of addressing the men, at Agra, of the 56th Regiment who were stationed there; and I have also had the pleasure of sending them a library of 850 volumes. A room has now been allotted to them to which they may go to this store of books instead of into the canteen.'

He collected £100 to assist the building of the Havelock Memorial Chapel where a room had been set aside for the soldiers to read. When he referred to his practical work in

India in a temperance speech at the Guildhall, he was already engaged in the collection of a second library to be despatched to another regiment. His charity was always practical. He arranged for the P. & O. and the East Indian railway to carry the books free of charge.

Lest it be thought that, aside from this act of charity, the Cooks' Indian connection has rested solely upon princes and pilgrims, it must be added that Mahatma Gandhi, though he preferred the ostentation of travelling third-class, always placed his arrangements with Cooks. Many a time Donald White at Victoria Station made a very special reservation in his own name in order to ensure complete privacy for the gentle Mahatma in his English journeys.

CHAPTER TWENTY-FOUR

Universal Expediency

It would be wrong to leave the impression that Thomas Cook's career was a stately steam progress from the Loughborough excursion to world success and fame. We have noticed already that there were disappointments and setbacks, occasions when a project had to be written off as a labour of love, dispirited moments even as late as the 'sixties when it had to be admitted that the future was quite obscure. Had there not been the brilliant and shrewd junior in the person of John Mason Cook, the whole Cook story might well have been different. Where one man sometimes failed, the other would succeed. If Thomas Cook himself disliked the East, his son and grandsons took to it with enthusiasm. When Thomas Cook had a leaning towards excessively large parties, his son was at hand to curb the dangerous tendency and to promote new ideas for individual travel. The progress towards the establishment of the Thomas Cook name as an international household word was, in fact, one of constant reorientation and of fits and starts.

Nowhere was this more so than in America, towards which Thomas Cook had looked with such eagerness before he had even set foot on the European continent. That his early dreams have been more than realized is evident from recent travel sales of nearly four million

pounds sterling over a single year in the United States, a
business second only to that in the United Kingdom. There
are now twenty-four Cook offices in the United States and
Canada, with about a thousand sub-agents. In a recent
year the firm booked about ten per cent of the visitors who
travelled to Britain from North America, paying over
five million dollars for their travel. Sales for travel within
the United States alone amounted to over five million
dollars and fifty-nine thousand people used Cooks to make
hotel reservations in North America. Some satisfaction
here for the ghost of Thomas Cook, who, in the flesh,
made those enthusiastic but disappointing exploratory
trips across the Atlantic in the 'sixties.

These, incidentally, were followed by a famous affair in
the 'seventies that had one unhappy sequel. This was the
visit in 1871 of a party of Knights Templar from Pittsburg,
gorgeous in their masonic paraphernalia, for a conducted
tour of Europe. They had been escorted by a hundred and
fifty of their fellows to New York where they joined the
Oceanic, then the last word in White Star liners. J. M.
Cook was waiting at Queenstown (Cobh) to take them
through Ireland and Scotland. Thomas Cook himself
greeted them in London, thence in the charge of couriers
they set out on a tour of Europe taking them as far south
as Naples and including the Passion Play at Oberammergau. Wherever they went they were welcomed by
fellow masons, and the detailed press accounts of their
journey carried Cook publicity all over America. All
members of the party enjoyed the prefix *Sir Knight* to their
names, and none was more enthusiastic about the travel
arrangements than their leader Sir Knight Jenkins. He
declared in fact that the Cook arrangements had impressed
him more than anything else in Europe and, before he
left for Queenstown and the *Oceanic* under the wing of
J. M. Cook, he made an offer to join the firm.

Thomas Cook, whose trusting nature could on occasion
be hoodwinked, accepted this and sent John Mason to

America shortly afterwards to familiarize the new partner with the mysteries of the business. Thus the firm of Cook, Son & Jenkins was established in New York, with branch offices in Boston, Philadelphia and Washington, and a separate office in London for the transaction of American business. The least that can be said of Sir Knight Jenkins was that he did not live up to expectations. The partnership did not last. The Cooks were horrified at the 'liberal and costly fashion' in which the New York office was managed and the fact that the rent alone amounted to one thousand two hundred pounds a year—a great sum for those days. It all ended by John Mason Cook pursuing the once glamorous Knight in the American Courts. The business seems to have been unaffected by this rumpus.

In spite of such disillusionments, Thomas Cook's appetite for the New World was undiminished. When the centenary of the Independence of the United States was celebrated by an International Conference in Philadelphia in 1876, he was present, both as temperance delegate and man of business. The British Commission had appointed him as its passenger agent for the Centennial Exhibition and his own travel bureau was conspicuous among the exhibits, while he himself was one of the delegates from Britain's National Temperance League. He gave fair measure to both interests as this short extract from his long enthusiastic report indicates: 'I could not absent myself from the business of our World's Ticket Office, on the Centennial Grounds, for more than a day and a half, but I had the pleasure of being present during the whole of the opening day, and again at a breakfast given to the delegates on the third day of the Convention.'

It took him half an hour to deliver the 'long and able address that had been consigned to him' by the League, but he noted with satisfaction that he was not called to order. At the breakfast, however, the speakers were limited to three minutes each, and here his eloquence got the better of him. He rode one of his favourite hobby-horses, the drinking of water on the Continent of Europe, and had to give way to cries of 'time' after twenty minutes.

From 1851 onwards, international congresses and exhibitions provided the Cooks with endless opportunities. Their history is indeed embroidered with the faded glories of these long-dead events. One of the more significant of these, in that it mingled both disappointment and triumph, was that held in Vienna in 1872. The Cooks had been approached by Baron Sir Anthony Rothschild, English Consul-General in Austria, to report to the Austrian Government on the transport and housing of Exhibition visitors. J. M. Cook paid a number of visits to Vienna and submitted a detailed report, only to find that the Austrians had floated a company of their own to carry out his ideas. The President of the Company, he noted with appropriate disgust, was a relative of an Austrian Minister of State.

He protested and prophesied failure, but he also set up in rivalry. His return fare from London to Vienna for exhibitors was only £4 1s. 9d., and he seems, in fact, to have treated competition in true nineteenth-century style. The Austrian concern collapsed a few days after the Exhibition opened, and it was found that the Cooks had in fact carried the bulk of the traffic. They might be Christian and ethical, but they meant business. Moreover, in the Cattle Show associated with the Exhibition, Queen Victoria was exhibiting valuable beasts and the Cooks were given the task of conveying these four-footed excursionists. It was the first time that they had been asked to deal with animals, but they were the last to refuse such new business, particularly when it emanated from the Palace. The cattle had to be conducted personally and with particular care so that they did not lose flesh in transit and had time to enjoy a rest before being shown. All this was accomplished. The name of Cook entered the household of the Widow of Windsor.

What was good enough, in fact, for the royal cattle

was good enough for Her Majesty's self. The Queen was among the many royal personages who made their travel arrangements with the Cooks. When the Queen began to travel privately to the French Riviera for the winter, Cook's discreetly made the arrangements and sent along a special courier to accompany the royal party. The Queen herself was evidently so satisfied with the courier that she appointed him to her own staff and King Edward VII afterwards employed him in this capacity. In Thomas Cook's lifetime, and indeed at the present day when the firm still handles the private travel arrangements of the old Queen's great-grandson, the Duke of Windsor, such arrangements are handled unobtrusively and with discretion. The ostentation of the late Kaiser's visit to the Holy Land was unique and a rare exception to the rule.

An occasion calling not only for tact but for security measures all too reminiscent of our own times concerned the Tsar of Russia. 'I had a private visit from a Gentleman-in-Waiting to Queen Victoria,' recollected the late Mr. Spiller, of Cook's, 'who told me that the Russian Royal Family were going to visit the Queen at Balmoral and we were to make the railway arrangements without advertising Thos. Cook & Son. I was given a royal carriage and I had to go to the navy and army people who had to send representatives to the Scottish port at which the visitors would arrive. It all had to be done very secretly because they were always afraid of trouble.

'About that time the manager of the Russian Railways told me that when the Russian Royal Family had to go anywhere they always had three trains ready, and no one knew by which one they would travel. Once the first train was bombed, but they were not on it.

'For a week I was going about from place to place making arrangements and planning things so that Queen Victoria should not be kept standing about any staircase at Balmoral waiting for her visitors. When I went to see the Russian Ambassador I wanted to get out of the carriage

CANNIBAL CHIEF (*releasing victim*):

'Why didn't you say before that you were from Cooks?—I'm their Local Agent.'

A COOK POSTER OF THE 1920'S.

and walk up to the door, but no, they must open the main gates for me. I was most anxious to find out which boat the Tsar was coming in, but the Ambassador said: *"Mon ami,* you will ask silly questions."

'In the end everything seemed to be arranged and I had gone home for a few hours' peace on Saturday afternoon when I received a telegram, "All arrangements cancelled." There was nothing to do but to get hold of the Prince of Wales, and the result was that the Queen sent a very stiff telegram to the Ambassador, who had been afraid to tell us of the change when we saw him. It turned out all right and Queen Victoria was not kept waiting on the steps.'

Personal foibles are not unknown to the Queen's descendants whom Cooks may be called upon to assist. King George V, an official guest at the Quirinal Palace in Rome in the 'twenties, sent for Cook's manager urgently and asked for some new sponges for his bath. Two cases were obtained 'on appro' from Roberts, the British chemists in Rome. The monarch made his choice, characteristically reminding Cook's that they were not to forget to charge them up. An incident not without charm concerned Princess Margaret's visit to Italy in 1949. The Cook office was officially concerned only with the handling of the royal luggage, but their advice was sought for a good restaurant where the royal party could stop for luncheon when travelling outside Rome by motor car. This advice being given and taken, Cooks telephoned the hotel proprietor to warn him to be ready to receive distinguished company. The delighted proprietor therefore had ample time to prepare a royal menu of distinction. Impressed perhaps by such preparations the Princess, before sitting down to table, asked to see the kitchens. There she observed in the background amid all the delicacies that had been prepared for her, the traditional pot containing the haricot beans and macaroni that the kitchen staff themselves would eat. It had to be tasted. It was so good that the Princess demanded it as a first course.

It was substantial, but she had a second helping. But for a small piece of cheese to follow, in fact, this was all she needed. The proprietor, unable to decide whether to feel complimented or crestfallen, was left with his elaborate royal menu untasted.

King Edward VII had personal foibles too. Landing from the royal yacht in 1906, he called at the Cook office at Naples and asked the manager to make arrangements for an excursion to Vesuvius, by that time well established as a Cook speciality. All the travel literature and the guide-books advised excursionists to travel out to the foot of the mountain by carriage. But His Majesty had just discovered a new zest for the internal combustion engine, and it was his royal command that he and the Queen should be conveyed to Vesuvius by motor car. In those days there were no cars, but the royal orders had been quite specific about transport, so, following the example of Thomas Cook on a former occasion in a Roman Holy Week, resort was made to the Italian nobility. After much search and a prolonged exchange of compliments, a brand new De Dion Bouton was found to take the royal couple as far as Cook's funicular railway.

Like the Nile steamers, this railway actually belonged to the Cooks and has remained in the hands of the firm until quite recently, when it was sold. Before it was built, Mark Twain in *The Innocents Abroad* complained about the 'native pirates' who would carry sightseers to the top of Vesuvius in sedan chairs. These 'pirates' were a force to reckon with even after the funicular had started, not very efficiently, to operate. John Mason Cook advanced money to the half bankrupt concessionaires who were the first operators and finally secured possession of it as the only means of ensuring his excursionists the promise to view the volcano. He came up against opposition every bit as determined as any he had encountered in India. He had to make good his right not only against litigants in the Italian Courts but also against 'the truculent mountaineers' themselves. These, it seems, had blackmailed the previous owners by extorting payment of £900 a year and a poll tax levied on every passenger. When Cook rejected their proposals, they attacked and burnt down the railway station, seized the rolling stock, threw the carriages down the old crater of the volcano and cut the line. Unintimidated, Cook repaired the line, but once more it was cut. Thereupon he closed down the whole concern for six months and refused to open it again until the local people, dependent as they were on tourists, felt the pinch and, to quote a contemporary account, were 'brought to their knees . . . glad enough to make friends.' They had ample opportunity for acclaiming Edward VII, for the upper part of the funicular to the crater had been destroyed by an eruption and the King, to their great delight, made the last stages of the journey on foot—no mean feat for one of his build.

In spite of their many services to many royalties, I doubt if the first two Cooks ever conceived that a reception by a reigning monarch would be included as part of a conducted tour. This, however, has several times been a feature of the Cooks African Safaris. In 1948, the King of Toro received a safari-excursion party in audience as they passed through Uganda. Another party was received by King Rudahigwa of the Watusi at the Royal Court at Nyanza. Even more fortunate were those who were regaled with champagne by the Emperor Haile Selasse in the Royal Palace at Addis Adaba in 1951, for each of them came away with a gold Coronation medal presented by the Emperor.

The pioneer Cook safari set out from London and ran from Cairo to the Cape in 1922. Others were organized from the United States in the 'thirties. But for a break during World War II, they have continued year by year. Nowadays they are largely airborne; and the direction has been reversed since the primitive native tribes and the wild life which are the main attraction are to be found less

in South Africa than formerly. So, by travelling Cape to
Cairo, the tour reaches its proper climax north instead of
south of the equator. They move with the smooth punctuality of their forerunner, the Loughborough-Leicester
excursion train, though they cater for other tastes—and
pockets. A 1952 quotation is for 11,550 miles in 77 days
at a cost of £1,354 14s. 6d.

It is not, I am told, by any means the dearest ticket you
can buy from Cooks. There are much more complicated
and luxurious journeys for those with deeper pockets. But
the policy that Thomas Cook developed and that is still
manifest is one of universal expediency. Whatever the
travel need, be it monetary or permanent, be it a camp
bed or an airliner sleeping berth, the organization must be
flexible enough to provide it or, if unobtainable, the next
best thing to it. Just as the old Cooks would buy a Nile
steamer or a mountain railway, accommodate royal cattle
or a megalomaniac Emperor, so the organization to-day
has gone into the holiday camp business and a scholastic
agency for the benefit of visitors and people overseas.
Universal world travel, paradoxically enough, seems to
have brought curtailment in freedom of movement. Old
Thomas Cook customers travelled far and wide without
much thought of passports and visas. So long as money
was in their pockets currency problems did not exist. If
they were sometimes haunted by fears of bandits, they at
least had nothing to fear from commissars. In that less
restricted world, freedom of movement developed slowly
following the march of steam. For the artisans and the
pilgrims as well as the newly-enriched middle-classes,
there were the Cooks at hand to arrange, organize, escort,
conduct and indeed to explain. Nevertheless, Thomas
Cook never meant to confine himself to conducted travel.
Then as now there were the needs of individuals to be met.
They served Mr. Gladstone just as their successors serve
Mr. Churchill on private travels. Many other famous
names crop up in the course of the years than I have been

able to mention—some passing by on pleasure, some on personal or official business. From all these records, let me select a complimentary note addressed from the Rue de Rivoli in Paris to Frank Henry Cook on April 1st, 1913: 'Dear Cook, Here is a little tale which may interest you, of what your people can do at a pinch. On Tuesday night we arrived, in the car, at Bourges from Marseilles and I was met by the news that the King of Greece would be buried at Athens on *Sunday* and it behoved me to get a room down there in time for the affair.

'Bourges is *not* what you might call a centre of civilization. It keeps one 10 c. time table and the leading hotel lights itself with candles. So I threw myself heavily, by telephone, into the arms of Cook Paris and demanded how I was to get from Bourges to Brindisi: Brindisi to Patras, and Patras to Athens in anything like time. If you know that corner of the Mediterranean you'll remember that the Greek & Italian steamer lines are sketchy and chaotic. At the same time as I telephoned Cook I wired practically duplicate inquiries to Reuter because it seemed to me utterly impossible that the various European representatives could by any means get from their capitals to Athens on the date given. Reuter (and this seems an additional feather in your cap) wired back: "Referring Cook bureau." Meantime Cook—who in this case was a man called Morton whom I'd met once before—telephoned me exhaustively that *on the dates given*, the thing was impossible by any known combination (he gave me the combinations) of Greek, or Italian boats. "You might just pull it off," he said, "by motoring to Nulon." In that, too, he was correct as I worked out afterwards. An hour or two later, when I had definitely abandoned the notion, Morton telephones again to tell me, *what Reuter should have done*, that the funeral was postponed till Wednesday; and presents me with two perfectly possible rail & boat combinations which should have landed me comfortably at Athens, via Patras (all hotels given) in ample time for the ceremony on the postponed date. That information was timely and tremendously useful to the man who had to go down in the long run.

'I don't suppose that this sort of thing is anything new to you but it pleased me as a client and an ex-journalist more than I can say.

'When I was at the Place de l'Opera this morning I asked how the thing was done. As far as I make out he'd dug up both the Greek and British embassies to get the second date *which Reuter didn't know* till Cook told him. In other words if I had depended on Reuter I should have been let down.

'There was a crispness and an accuracy about the whole thing that I can't help boring you with.

'Mrs. Kipling joins me in kindest regards to you both and I am

Very sincerely and gratefully yours

RUDYARD KIPLING.'

CHAPTER TWENTY-FIVE

A Travellers' Cheque for Dreamland

As soon as travel entails the crossing of frontiers, problems of money begin. The earliest of Cook excursionists, as we have seen, sometimes pawned their watches to raise a fare. Others offered their watches to the ever-trusting Thomas Cook, when they went short of cash. As soon as foreign currency was involved, however, the Cooks were obliged to consider serving the needs of their customers' pockets, as well as providing tickets. Nowadays the financial departments take up more space than any other in the firm's headquarters. Cook's travellers' cheques and hotel vouchers are honoured throughout the world. During the post-war years of currency restriction, British customers have been able to make all their often elaborate financial arrangements with the British Treasury through the firm's *Exchange Control Department* in London.

The Cooks at first took to banking and currency exchange with a certain reluctance. Yet already in 1879 it was so important that it had become a unit distinct from the general business, and during the latter part of the nineteenth century it continued to extend so that the Cooks not only acted as general bankers but as foreign bankers issuing their own drafts and currency notes and remitting money by cable throughout the world.

Henry Spiller, who joined the firm in 1873, eventually

becoming Chief Negotiator and remaining patriarchially associated with the business till his death at the age of ninety-two in 1938, was the first to press John Mason Cook to develop the banking side. In a letter from Cairo dated 1892, John Mason rejected his proposals on the grounds of lack of capital: '. . . My present idea is that I have plenty of capital for our general business without the B. & E. dept. therefore if really necessary, I must draw in rather than expand the B. & E. dept. But if you can find £10,000 to extend that dept. I am quite prepared to receive a definite proposal . . .'

Another letter to Spiller from Arthur Faulkner, who became Cook's financial manager, indicates that John Mason was understandably reluctant to deviate his interest from the all-absorbing affairs of the Middle and Far East: '. . . You sometimes complain in my absence that there is little or no interest taken in the B. & E.—well it is a pet child of ours . . . but I think Mr. John Cook . . . has so much to think about in the tourist business that he cannot devote much time to that but . . . he has decided to bring his son Ernest up to that branch of the business.'

Banking and foreign exchange soon ceased to be regarded as a lucrative sideline and Cook's were one of the world's most widely used *bureaux de change*. Mr. A. S. Jenkinson, who for many years has specialized in the firm's international finance, recollects that early in this century, when currency was still blessedly free in London, many of the banks which advertised a foreign currency service relied upon a neighbouring Cook's office for the cash. 'It was a standing joke with our cashiers that branch banks kept their clients waiting while a cashier slipped out of the bank's back door and hurried round to the nearest Cook's to change money. In the 'twenties, while members of the family were still running the business, it was converted into two separate limited companies, one to deal with travel, the other with bank activities. The subsequent history of the firm, first its control by Wagons-

Lits, then the return of control to the British railways, has naturally modified the complex pattern of this branch of the business, but not decreased it. In a recent year travellers cheques were sold to the value of ten million sterling with a further five and three-quarter million in dollar cheques.

By way of postscript to this tale of high finance, it is fitting perhaps to mention a letter received just after the unveiling ceremony at Thomas Cook's birthplace in 1952. It was written by the grand-daughter of John Astle, a Melbourne market gardener 'in a very humble way' who was an early friend of Thomas Cook. It recalls an occasion when Cook borrowed £100 in order to buy a wagonette 'to travel somewhere Ilkeston way.' The money was repaid; but what, asks this correspondent, was the story of the transaction?

Cook, though he told us so much about his early strivings and his later travels, left no record of that; and the archives, though they tell of many a horse-drawn journey, are silent. He was as proud of his humble origin as he was of his evangelical background. In his eightieth year he delighted in the recollection not of his royal or wealthy clients but of such a one as Mrs. Mary Pegg of Melbourne who sold her jewellery and trinkets to clear the General Baptist Chapel from debt. 'It was my pleasure to serve that lady when a little boy, going every day to the Greenhill pump for water for drinking and culinary purposes.'

The obsession with water was nobly conceived and meticulously served. It may well have killed John Mason Cook. He was in indifferent health when the Kaiser's visit to the Holy Land was being planned, and, as we know, the arrangements were deputed to his eldest son Frank. Nevertheless he felt obliged, in the words of *The Excursionist*, 'to accompany his Majesty . . .' He came back to his newly-acquired mansion, Mount Felix, at Walton-on-Thames, only to die. Some said it was the Palestine heat.

Many, however, pointed to the fact that he alone of the party persisted in drinking water instead of wine. He had been present—and his father had been still living, blind, proud and infirm—when the Cook jubilee was celebrated in 1891 with a banquet at the Hotel Metropole in London. Three royalties honoured the occasion, Prince Edward of Saxe Weimar, Prince Henry of Battenberg, and the Duke of Cambridge who recalled the Soudan campaign in responding to the toast of the Army.

'. . . it almost nightly happens,' wrote Thomas Cook in that same year, 'that in the first part of the night, while I sleep somewhat heavily, I am engaged in my dreams in various matters of work connected with tours and travels, and I make many trips through dreamland which leave an impression upon me in the wakeful hours of the morning . . .' Such were the good dreams of a nineteenth-century worthy who never did anyone any harm. Indeed they said of him at the time of his death that he had 'really contributed, in no small degree, to deliver middle-class English people from insular narrowness of mind, from stupid and silly antipathy to foreign nations, the effect of sheer ignorance. . . .'

Middle-class English? Perhaps a cavalcade, including mill-hands, Indian potentates, teetotal evangelists, safari-excursionists, European royalties, American masonic nobility, Mecca pilgrims, suggests a wider range? No doubt *The Times*, seeking a more perspective view of their former globe-girdling correspondent, was right in referring to the inclination to take a "too lofty view of . . . service to humanity.' Even so it went on to grant judicially that 'such a natural exaggeration is easily pardoned.'

My own Cook's excursion started at a humble brick semi-detached cottage in Melbourne on a sultry summer afternoon. It ended in Bath on a sparkling autumn morning at No. 1, Sion Hill Place, a mansion of more than twenty rooms and surely unique in semi-detachedness.

I had spanned three generations. It was Mr. Ernest

Cook, aged eighty-seven, the only surviving grandson of Thomas, who opened the front door and, with something of the meticulous air of his forebears, congratulated me upon being there punctually on time. This last of the Cooks to work in the business has devoted the long years of his retirement to the æsthetic matters which the grandfather hardly had time to contemplate except where they were to be noted by his ever-prolific pen in one of his many guide-books or notes for travellers. Mr. Ernest Cook, a bachelor who lives alone and no longer entertains, and who indeed is often described in the Press as a recluse, has spent a quarter of a century devoting himself with much of his grandfather's public spirit to two hobbies—paintings and period architecture. His travels in Persia or Australia, his early working life under the strict regime of John Mason Cook, are in his great age almost forgotten.

As I entered his home, so unlike any semi-detached house not only because of the grandeur of its hillside aspect overlooking Bath, but also because of its 136-acre private park, he indicated two sets of Gainsborough water-colours let into the panel of the door. He had warned me by letter that, though we might speak of the affairs of his grand-father, it would also take at least an hour to see the pictures. Across the end of the house he has caused to be added the spacious salons and the long façade of a famous eighteenth-century mansion which was demolished. Here the great windows look out over terraces and trim park. Even a cursory inspection of the paintings and period furniture took more than the hour he had suggested. Few guests now enjoy this unusual combination which mingles the urbanity of England's most stately city with the spacious atmosphere of an English landed estate.

It will be enjoyed by people in the future. For Mr. Cook has formed a Trust under the terms of which this, together with six estates totalling 13,215 acres in Buckinghamshire, Berkshire, Leicestershire and Gloucestershire, are to be maintained and used for educational purposes. He has already presented Boarstall Tower and the magnificent sixteenth-century Montacute, with its 303 acres, to the National Trust. There are also three estates, Buscot beside the Thames, Bradenham in Buckinghamshire, and Coleshill, a treasure only recently destroyed by fire. We can be sure at least that these will not suffer the fate of Thomas Cook's memorial to daughter Annie in the City of Leicester—a commentary upon the many changes of fortune possible in the span of three generations.

Thomas Cook's authentic memorial is not only his almhouses and the modest plaque on the cottage at Melbourne, but a household word of world renown. It is an unexpected twist that his name should be perpetuated by a grandson in the endowment of a treasure which, but for the public spirit of such men as Ernest Cook, would vanish with the progress of this age.

Index

251